Shavannah Angelique's debut poetry collection, *Freed Bird: Dancing from Flower to Fruit,* was the start to a personal, yet cathartic love story. The self-love anthem ultimately won the 2021 Distinguished Author's Guild Poetry Award.

From there, she continues to write poetry that alters perspective for the better, focusing on introspection and self-growth. Whether those stories are personal, or someone else's, she continues to speak volumes to feelings of true depth.

To everyone who believed in Hazel and Noah and saw them
before they saw each other; as well as those who loved me
along the way.

Shavannah Angelique

ENDLESSLY, I'LL LOVE YOU

AUSTIN MACAULEY PUBLISHERS™
LONDON • CAMBRIDGE • NEW YORK • SHARJAH

Ordering Information
Quantity sales: Special discounts are available on quantity purchases by corporations, associations, and others. For details, contact the publisher at the address below.

Publisher's Cataloging-in-Publication data
Angelique, Shavannah
Endlessly, I'll Love You

ISBN 9798891551640 (Paperback)
ISBN 9798891551657 (ePub e-book)

Library of Congress Control Number: 2023922380

www.austinmacauley.com/us

First Published 2024
Austin Macauley Publishers LLC
40 Wall Street, 33rd Floor, Suite 3302
New York, NY 10005
USA

mail-usa@austinmacauley.com
+1 (646) 5125767

Table of Contents

Existing

I could feel things very deeply for one of three reasons:

1. I'm a woman

ridden with emotions that are as
active as the sea
as buoyant and as fluid, a spectrum
from calm to raging

2. A hopeless romantic

who hangs on
words the way that an octopus
pushes oxygen to her young, until
her dying breath, and until there's
nothing left

3. I'm a writer

crafting worlds from words, a
photographer sees the most minute
details, a singer hears pitches and

each octave they can differ, a
sculptor feels every wrinkle and
vein, a florist floats from scents
alike and new—from roses to geraniums to violets blue, a
chef
creates art for your tongue, a
balancing act of sweet and savory.
I take all of that and create a
love story.

Or maybe it's that I'm all three, inevitably fated to feel everything.

My hands don't hold much these days. Tools at work, a greasy burger from time to time, or drink to wash down the monotony that life can become sometimes. My friends always tell me that I should get back out there after my ex, but I hear them say that at the same time I see them arguing with their girlfriends and complaining about their headaches.

I'm not sure I want to sign up for that again. My hands used to hold on to someone that I thought loved me the way I very much loved her. I was willing to be all in with her, but she had other plans.

She didn't paint the picture of what love was supposed to be naturally; instead, she painted a picture of what love was under dire and demanding circumstances. That if I loved her, I would do whatever it took, and she so freely tested just how far my love would carry—still, I would fail every time.

It wasn't until I caught her with someone that my love decided it wouldn't be carried to that level of forgiveness. So, I swore off it, and swore off her. I was an addict, now 2 years sober, and she was the drug. She wouldn't ever get love from me again, and I was never tempted by her taste.

Ultimately, love should have never been a test, had it been real, I would have never been in a position where I had to fight for it, had to beg for it, and had to hurt from it. Love would have never asked me for those things. I think that's why it was finally so easy for me to walk away, and even easier to stop wanting to try.

When I look around, I see people hurting in their relationships, sacrificing, and compromising on their boundaries and self-respect. I saw my mother get hurt by my father's absence, and my sister was left because she no longer fit the bill of a selfish and egotistical man.

I saw my friends get used and cheated on. And then there's me, the first night going out in six months because my responsibilities seemed to flood my calendar. As I finished off my second old fashioned, my friend told me again, "you should go talk to that girl, man. She's hot. You never know, man, she could be the one."

I looked over to find eyes that were glued to my group of friends, her gaze bouncing off each one of us, contemplating who would be the one to get her a free drink that night—her self-tanning lotion glistened in the dimmed lounge lights.

"Nah man, I'm good on that one. Maybe for you though." And the group laughed as someone else changed the subject. After my ex, I had no interest in shallow, overly social, or narcissistic. If I'd ever find the one, and that's a big if, she wouldn't be in a place like this.

I don't even want to be in a place like this anymore. I'd imagine she would be a rare find in a common place, a grocery store or the line at the bank. She would be extraordinary in an ordinary setting.

If I thought really hard about it, I could picture that my future was peaceful because I was lucky enough to find peace in human form. So, I try my hardest not to think about it.

But that was all behind me now. It'd been quite some time since I had that hanging over my head. Not that I imagine I will actually fall in love again, but if I did, I think that it will be far away into the future. And if I did, she will be nothing like the past.

I never imagined what my future would look like. But if I had to put something onto paper, I'd say something deep. Something steady, something calm. Maybe along the way I lost the definition of what love is, but I know for certain what it's not. I think that's enough for me.

So, it'd been a while since my hands had held something, even longer since my heart had.

I find myself speaking to the universe and laying out my terms
This is what I choose
Go find me this love and if nothing comes about
Then I shall rest in my own company and be sufficient without
For my body is no longer a sacrifice for part time connections
Because my body is what's telling me to find a love that, too, believes in lifetime ties, sweetly interconnected truths.
The times I sit and look inward, I see strength and a stubborn lover
One that doesn't let me shut down when I succumb to the dark abyss, I once called home
But instead looks me deep inside my glossy eyes and holds me in his arms tight
I see laughter that somehow erases the past that is painted vividly in my rear view
So lifelike, it could have been a movie
I see slow and steady waters that gently touch the shore
Never asking for what I can't give, never asking for more
Our bodies intertwined while we breathe in each other's presence
This aroma, your candor, I admire all of your essence.

Rivers stopped flowing in my mind
Time stopped ticking, too
No matter how quickly I began walking
My feet, forcing the earth to turn on its axis
And yet
Minutes slowed to a halt and the sun beat me into a
sweltering submission
Life was unwound tapes, stuck in the VCR
But there was no pencil handy to fix it
There was this:
The sun rises, I follow suit
The sun shines, I try to, too
Hydrate and work
Work and continue
I dance and become in tune
With the earth and with some people too
I love, but I keep that one for me, too
I eat, I breathe, I read
I sleep
And when the sun calls
I come too
Do I yet share this cycle with another
Or am I just a lonely dancing fool
Do I share my love

Or do I keep that to myself
It's a hefty price and someone could steal away at that too
I eat, I breathe, I sleep
And when the sun calls, I come too.

I get lost and hope to find no one
I feel like it's an opportunity to learn
It's a chance to love
It's a moment to live
And I decided in my healing
That I deserve to live
I deserve to love
I deserve to learn
No matter how scary it may be
It could never have fangs bigger than the monsters that tried
to defeat me
So, I get lost and hope to find no one
I live in my day-to-day solitude, but I renamed it solace
The beauty is in understanding that at the end of the day
The home that is me is well taken care of.

48 weeks now, coasting
Car set on auto cruise
Nothing but me, my music, and the view
Never feeling the need to adjust my routine
I was coasting
The most unideal way to live life
Coasting, missing things
May as well have my eyes shut
While someone else is in the driver's seat
If it wasn't for the air in my lungs
I'd have to investigate if my heart still had a beat
By the time the sun goes down
I find myself in a bed that I return to, feeling beat
Each day has been a battle, and sometimes I lie with defeat
I've been coasting
I wonder what would happen if I stopped off the coast to just see
Maybe it's time I take some time to just breathe
Take some time for me
Explore what else exists beyond the coast for me.

I loved you
But I thought love was deeper than lust
I thought love was deeper than the way you liked to be
fucked
Deeper than the way you like your back rubbed
I loved you ten toes down
Do anything for you, regardless of who was around
I loved you to the core that I always kept warm for you
Loved you to the moon, the pendant I bought and adorned
on you
I loved you
But you didn't think love was deeper than the honey on your
skin
It was surface level
A first-degree burn
Not even deep enough to leave a scar in the end
So, my love for you that once lasted, now hangs in the tree
planted in the yard
Left it there for you
Cause obviously
It wasn't meant for me anymore.

I don't think I realized how mundane of a life I lived. I wasn't enjoying anything because I was so hell-bent on protecting my peace that I shut everyone out. I shut out all the possibilities of new people, new relationships, new anything.

I knew, or somehow, I decided that if I never let anyone in again, I would never get hurt. But that's not what was happening here. Because I don't think that avoidance of pain or potential risk factors actually decreased the chance of getting hurt.

Here I was, existing through this cycle where sometimes I saw my friends, but mostly I stayed to my work schedule. There was no shame in it, because I enjoy what I do, but there was also no spark in it. There was no drive behind my actions, it was like somewhere along the way I had lost my motivation.

I was stuck, and I felt that. But I also felt the desire to change something in my life to find that light again. To find my motivation again. Maybe in a book, maybe in a song, but it needed to be something different than what I was already doing.

Hands that hold empty promises under the midnight moon
Feel so heavy each time I remember you
The crevice of my palms remembers that night you fell asleep in my arms
And the fingertips, lined with the very essence of me
Remembers the way your lips feel before you'd kiss me
But most of all
My hands remember the night I let you go
After having walked on my heart
And took it apart
Love was a game to you
And somehow the man attached to those palms became a pawn
Now, my hands hold empty promises
But now I'll let those go too.

I can't stand walking around this world, sometimes it feels so pointless to be here. *People* are as altered as they come; just as much altered in real life as they are on social media. You don't know who is who or what they stand for.

You don't know what they love, but you certainly know what they hate. You can't tell what makes people smile, and it's suddenly taboo to openly ask someone; it's taboo to care. No one fucking *cares* anymore.

This world fills me with angst and anxiety, I counter it as much as I can but I'm only human. I'm just a man. So, I mostly stay to myself a lot. I have a few friends, anything more than three solid people is just excessive.

I visit my family when I can, and I work. I have gone through plenty, I've seen enough, and I really don't have the energy or capacity to take on more. I've had my share of love-adjacent adventures and I ultimately wonder if the relationships failed because of me and my issues, because of the women I chose in uncertain times, or simply the fact that we were incompatible.

Two puzzle pieces from different boxes, never meant to touch surfaces. Although longing to connect to someone, it was forced in the end. Maybe that's why, maybe my list of lovers that never worked out exists because they were cut from the wrong puzzle and it was a forced connection, when everyone deserves to find their connecting piece.

The one that nestles into the contours of their bodies and creates a vision where you were once blinded. *Maybe that's why.*

I did see this one girl at a library a couple of weeks back, she was something else, she made me wish I was less of myself, and more open to trying something new. She seemed serene, which was already an anomaly in this chaotic world.

I don't know if she was quiet because she was being respectful and libraries thrive on little old ladies shushing everyone who walks in; or if she was being quiet because she, too, preferred her world inside, rather than what we walk through on the outside.

I decided that she seemed nice and even felt it when I accidentally bumped into her shoulder as I was reaching for a novel. She turned to me for the slightest second, and I saw the most beautiful eyes I had ever seen in my life.

They were dark, but still glowing. And after I apologized, she then smiled a small smile and said, "Don't sweat it." Her voice was like velvet. She went back to focusing on what she was looking for and her hair fell back down like the thick curtain it was, covering her gorgeous eyes and inviting smile.

Then she left and I was a fool for not saying more. For not telling her that my name was Noah. For not saying I'd love to buy her coffee. For not saying a word else. *Man, she was beautiful.*

I headed to the front and checked out my book that I never read in the end. It sat on my dresser collecting dust, just waiting to be returned because I never put it to good use. Even the book knew I was a fool. I spent the rest of the day lost in the shine of her eyes.

I don't know why I was so distracted over this five second exchange. And then she went back to what she was doing as if it never happened. I wonder what music was playing in her headphones.

I wondered what movie she would like to go see if I had the courage to ask her out. I wondered what her name might be and how well it would sound rolling off my lips. But in my hesitation and cowardice, I didn't ask her any of those questions.

I was a deer caught in headlights and froze at the sight of her. So, I suppose I would never know, just my luck.

***

Eventually, I made my way back to the library to return the books I had checked out a few weeks ago. I prepared myself for the little old lady to ask how it was and if I had enjoyed it.

Surely, I'd say yes, I loved it. I might even check out more of his work. *She doesn't have to know that I never even cracked it open.* The little old lady didn't care if I read them or not, she got paid either way, but I still wanted it to seem like my effort and intentions were aligned with my checking out books in the first place.

And there she was when I walked in, I must have been the luckiest fool in the world. The girl with the dark eyes and the serene smile, hair as thick as theater curtains. Where

I was going to return one unread book, she was returning three—none of which were neglected like mine, I'd guess.

This time, bypassing the return desk, I walked up to her, *I wasn't going to be a fool twice,* and I looked at her, I extended my hand so quickly, it could have easily been mistaken for an attack, though I was aiming for a handshake gesture and said, "I'm Noah."

Her eyes grew so wide, and her spine straightened out. Surely, she was wondering why this random dude was talking to her, and why did he want to shake her hand. Surely, she was a little caught off guard because I was a tower in comparison to her small frame.

I wasn't graceful in my introduction to her; I didn't appear to be smooth and well-put together. As much as I pondered on what I would say to her, none of it mattered because it all went out the window.

My nerves were showing deep in the laugh lines around my smile. I hoped she wouldn't notice, but I felt them loudly and most certainly in the forefront of my appearance. I always smiled when I was nervous.

Surely, despite my best efforts, I was a fool again but I would rather be a fool that tried to meet those gorgeous eyes and beautiful smile, then be the fool who failed twice.

I just don't think I've ever seen a brilliance like you
Exuding light through your smile the way you do
And your eyes glisten like honey in the sun
And suddenly, I'm a fool
Tell me what I need to do
To learn what makes you happy
And learn what feeds your soul
Because I want to live that deep in your life
I want to be the reason you smile so bright

You deserve to be soft again
Like fleece lined blankets that cover you in winter storms
Soft, like a pillowy comforter that makes clouds envious
You deserve to be curious without remorse
Playful without precaution
Daring without fear
And loving without reprimand
You deserve a heart to carry yours and whisper sweet
nothings
Until the sun rises and, too, rests on your cheek until you
wake of warm kisses
You deserve to hold happiness until your knuckles ache at
grasping onto it so long
But don't let go
Because you deserve to have joy until the happiness is
absorbed into the beds of your nails
So deep so, that everything you touch from that moment on
is also illuminated with bliss
So much so, that you become the happy that people envision
in goals
You deserve love so forgiving that you learn to forgive
yourself for your shortcomings
A love that tells you to stop looking backward
Because your future is calling for you

A love that creates solace in moments once furrowed
And ease in memories tense
You deserve a love that brings you peace
Always potentially giving more, but never anything less.

Sometimes, when no one is paying me any amount of attention, I close my eyes and envision the lyrics to my favorite song dancing on the screen in my mind. I can hear the music and I just get lost in the words that once lulled me to sleep on restless nights.

It separates me from the stress that I sometimes feel. Life has been very generous in making sure that I have plenty of lessons to learn. So, every morning, I insist on playing my favorite songs, I insist on dancing in moments where I feel like no one is watching.

For the most part, I think I am pretty successful at doing it when no one is around; not because I am shy, but because I may be the world's worst dancer, I can't carry a tune anywhere in my body.

I have long since left behind the adolescent dreams of being the next greatest singer or choreographer. Instead, I think that when I grow up—in the metaphorical sense in which I feel I am at my prime and I have achieved my goals—I would have become a counselor to distraught teens.

That could very well be a bad idea, after all, I was a distraught teen. Maybe it's that I was desperate to fit in, desperate for approval. I would do things that my heart knew weren't right, but I would do them anyways because there was a stamp of validation at the end of the tunnel.

There were welcoming sounds of laughter and *friends* who would accept me as I was. Only, I wasn't acting like myself in order to get there. I could feel myself not being authentic, and somehow that snowballed into poor choices.

My parents saw it as rebellion, I knew it as confusion. It wasn't until later in life that I decided to fall back and fall into myself. I'm more comfortable here, more me than ever.

So, I danced in the corners of my mind when no one was watching. And when they were, I smiled toward them and hoped it did something to brighten their day or maybe they thought I was weird. And that was okay too.

Right now, I read a lot of books, and there wasn't one genre that I favored more than the others. It was just a totally different world, and I love that. It was a place where nothing bad had ever happened—so I explored them quite frequently.

There was a small library around the corner from my apartment that I visited, the librarian—Eloise—was a sweet old lady. If she shushed anyone else, she was going to earn herself a reputation by meeting all the librarian stereotypes; she'd quiet them anyway.

Today, I was perusing the stacks near the middle of the library, about three rows from the bottom, not low enough to where I needed to stoop, but still low enough to where I needed to bend.

In this moment, I wished I had tied my hair up this morning, it kept falling and blocking my view, making me forget what I was even looking for. Yet, I kept looking anyway.

This very tall guy bumped into me, I tended to be invisible some days, which was no one's fault at all. So, I looked up, smiled—hoping it brightened someone's day, and also hoping that I didn't look weird—and said something that wasn't worth remembering at all.

In the split second that I picked my head up enough for my hair to unblock my view and smile, I saw that the guy that bumped into me wasn't just some standard, run of the mill looking guy. He was actually really handsome.

Handsome is reserved for the type of guys who are more than just cute on the outside, but seemingly decent, respectable even. The moment lasted all of two seconds, but I thought of him the entire time I was grabbing at random books and checking them out.

I almost hoped that he would run into me again, maybe he would knock over the stack of books in my arms and meet me on the floor to collect them. We would laugh and he would ask for my name.

But this wasn't a rom-com and I was not the love interest in some overly scripted movie. Like I said, sometimes I tended to be invisible, and these were moments that I wished I wasn't, because he was really handsome.

I feel so consumed by my own cloud of hesitation some days that I genuinely don't know if the sun is shining or if it's raining. What if love looked at me today and I was none the wiser?

Would I even know its scent if a breeze took it by my nose? And how does a creature of habit even change its ways? They say it takes 90 days to change your life, but if on day 89, I back out, can I go back to my safe shell, the hermit that I am?

Or will I then be open to everything that's to come, will I be open to love and all that it brings? Because if memory serves me correctly, it could often bring me pain.

Love could sometimes be disguised as beauty, making me want to reach day 89, and then on that 91st day, when I am a changed woman, a more loving woman, a more invested woman, love can take off his mask and reveal what I had feared long ago.

But I will already be changed, already be loving, already be invested. Then what? Wasn't my hesitation stitched into my bones to protect me from crying in nights alone? Like many moons ago, when I used to cry into my pillow. I loved, and to think I could ever do that again; another past tense ending.

I just feel as though, maybe I should learn to walk with my hesitation. I'd love to get to know its name and favorite color, but also its fears and admirations.

I think it's the unknown that scares me most, and that's the number one thing that I can't control. With any temptation or new face, there is always going to be something I don't know. But if one thing is for certain, I know that I can't go back to the way it was, so it's either face the unknown or remain alone.

Sometimes, I just don't know. There's nothing wrong with single made dinners, the two plants that line the mantle, and the record player in my home. There's nothing sad, nothing sorry, nothing needing changing.

So, I believe my fear of the unknown is big because it means risking this beautiful peace that I worked hard to grow. I planted each tear in the soil until a root started to grow.

I watered it with affirmations that I was going to be okay, and to my surprise, I woke to blooms that were colored the same color as my eyes and shape as my smile. My hesitation lay deeper than what instantly showed.

I love, love, but I love even more the things I had grown, and I wouldn't want to danger those beautiful growing bulbs.

I think I could be really good at falling in love again
If you don't mind the need for reassurance
The walls that, at first, might make you nervous
The pause in my spine when your fingers reach for mine
The hesitation in my voice when you say you want me
The marathon I will run to try and find my ability to trust
The insomnia and desperate plea for sweet dreams
Or even my tendency to float with the wind
As it carries me away
I think I could be really, really good at falling in love
someday.

Did you know that I'm Libra?
Known to be the romantic
Self-indulgent one
So, let me indulge
Be my guilty pleasure
As I dip my finger in your sweet, cool whipped skin
Lick and go back in
Can't think now, I'll regret you in the morning
I'm an air sign
So, I drift in and out of lust and love
As easily and quickly as the breeze turns cold
I weigh in the side of love more often than I'd care to admit
And that is why I find myself at a cold pause, once again
With you
Wanting you
For you
To love you or to lust you
Make it make sense in my head
Make it make sense as I push you to my bed
Let me take out my scales
And weigh my options instead
Pros against a handful of cons
Let me see if I can make loving you a balance

Like the way the sun rises over the mountain tops, breaking night and day giving us dawn

Pro: You taste as sweet as honey chamomile tea

When the taste of you dances on my tongue, I grin and smile sweetly.

Pro: You calm and excite me

Like a long embrace immediately after exiting a roller coaster ride

You give me calms after joining me in my highs.

Con: You're awfully real

You have the ability to grab me by the heart and control when the blood pumps

But don't make my heart skip a beat

I want you, but I want you steadily.

Pro: I love the way my hand feels in yours

Like safe is a new feeling and apparently, I've never felt safe before.

Con: What if you're a liar?

What if the way you say I'm special and the way you call me babe

Is all just a ruse to get me in bed or to get your way?

Con: I'm just waiting for you to walk away, cause you'll get tired of my need for your home-like embrace

And me calling it my safe space

Your arms, my saving grace

Next thing I know, you're walking and walking away.

Con: My heart can't take another break

And it looks like I can't do this

See, my scales don't make mistakes

See, this is what it means to think with my heart

See, logically, I know that my list of cons that weigh me
down
That slowly hold me back
Are very much fabricated
I know what ifs aren't real
See, I know this
And I also know that trusting in you and trusting in love
could heal
Each plate of my scales is stacked so high,
But it is cons that are overflowing
And ultimately weighing down
And ultimately undoing
All the feelings I have felt in my longing for you
The breeze carries me
Once again, over that hill
That separate love and lust
Classic Libra
Overthinking
Until love turns to dust.

I recall being in love once in my life. My entire body was invested in the scent and essence of one man, I could have loved him for the rest of my life if my gut had let me. I was young and set into tunnel vision, wishing to bloom a future that only the two of us would be in, maybe some children of our own with a house that we built.

I insisted that love have legs this time, I insisted that it carry us in strides and any rough patches we would hurdle over together. So, I learned forgiveness and colored it the same color blue as his eyes because it was every time that I looked at his, frowned downward and strong that I mustered up the strength to forgive his shortcomings.

His outward bursts and anger, I would forgive every time. A deep ocean blue, so deep that once I fell in the waters of his eyes, I never stopped swimming because I couldn't get out. He would be late and blue forgiveness would spill from my lips.

He shouted, but not at me, and blue forgiveness would leak from my eyes. He painted me with names that didn't belong to me, and blue forgiveness would rush from my arms as I reluctantly held him in his apologies. He threw plates across the room, never aiming them at me, and blue forgiveness became my tired heart.

He screamed at me to do better, be better, and reminded me this is why I never had better; I was lucky to have this kind of *better* in my sheets—and I thanked him for being my version of better right now by offering him the last bit of blue forgiveness I had. I thought love was supposed to be forgiving, so I painted the whole damn world blue.

I stopped trusting my gut when he was in my presence because he yelled louder than the cringing I felt in my torso. My body would tell me in ways that I would always ignore that he wasn't love and I wasn't in it.

My lips would tremble when my heart tried to speak, my knees would quiver when my jaw got tense. I stopped looking up at the sky when I walked. I stopped speaking to myself with love and he stopped telling me that he loved me, said I should just know that he does, or else why would he be here?

If he didn't love me, then why would he care? If he didn't love me, then why would he fight so much to get it right? But if he loved me, then why would he fight so hard in the first place? I'm not sure that love is supposed to be that loud.

I wanted my heart to dance with his, the way it did when we were younger, when our hearts first met. I would smile and he always placed his thumb at the corner of my lips, as to hold my smile for safekeeping. He once said it was the reason that he fell in love with me.

Second was my eyes. Always big and bright, he would say, like stars. Third was the way I cared for him. He never felt love before meeting me and when I was around, he was filling in a void that had since been empty. He siphoned the love from my bones, and I was weaker because of it.

I kept shutting out the noises in my head that were saying this wasn't love, but instead I was creating a love that I wanted it to be. I let him off the hook by disregarding my needs and in the end, he got years of my time, all of my love, and now occupies a space in my mind that constantly needs reassurance.

I have been sitting with myself ever since, sometimes in solitude and sometimes in loneliness that resulted in a poor choice of company. I picked out a new color for forgiveness because I didn't want him to have that remnant as well, I wanted to forgive myself, and I didn't want his deep ocean blue on my body ever again.

Green. I forgave myself in shades of green, like a beautiful plant sprouting for the first time, growing healthy and big. Green on my eyes for ever looking down when I walked. Green on my body for ever sharing it with someone who didn't appreciate every single flaw that covered it.

Green in my mind for thinking that I deserved the words he once told me. That act of forgiveness is ongoing because some days, I still hear them, loud and clear, and struggle to take it apart.

I find that some days, my muscles are too weak to deconstruct the hatred he had placed on me, and I end up walking through the day thinking he was right when he said that his angry, selfish love was the one I deserved.

I needed to forgive myself for ever allowing that in my life, and most of all, I needed to forgive myself for ignoring my screams. My intuition tried so hard to tell me, but I didn't listen.

I wanted love, but he was a wolf in sheep's clothing. I wanted love, but he was hard, in soft packaging. I wanted love, but he was a lesson.

Some days, I don't think I will ever be cut out to love again, because I gave all of my love in its entirety. He depleted me of it. I didn't even have love for myself, I had to go find it in nature and breathe it in.

I had to see love from afar and mimic its movements, hoping my muscles remember the scene by the end of the day. And after a long night's rest, I woke up in the morning trying to reiterate the same movements, I try to see if I am love yet.

I rehearsed it in the mirror and drank it down along with my vitamins, trying hard to get back to healthy love. How could I ever share that again when it'd taken so much to get it back?

How could I allow myself to be so naive with my heart and frivolous with my love as to share it with someone whose intentions I did not know? Even though I want to love, love again and swim in someone's eyes again and hold someone's hand as their hand holds mine.

So, I continued to look for love in all the right places, this time. I looked in cups of coffee, in beautiful flowers, and in songs that were only sad because they reminded me of what I didn't have.

I looked for love in the mirror, but I didn't always see it there—I checked for it consistently anyways, even on days when tears insisted on falling down my cheeks. I looked for love in art and books, I looked for love in the scents that were carried on the breeze.

You ever met a woman that came with an advisory label?
So, you know what you're getting yourself into, right from
the jump?
So, you know that she's a mess, right from day one?
So, you know that she's a little bit broken, that she's kind
of coming undone?
You ever met a woman who says it like it is
That she gets a little needy
A little bit dismissive
That she's fighting a war inside her chest
Because she's in the middle of redefining who she is
That dismisses her own feelings, calls herself irrational
Paints herself the demon
Because she sees the good in other people
You ever met someone who falls so hard in love
Yet, never knew the feeling
Everything she's ever wanted
Has just been a dream, and
She gives and tries
Trips on the heartstrings
Shows up with bloodied knees
Just to try again at loving
Have you ever met a woman who tells you first thing
That she's got a hair trigger reaction

Too often, sometimes small things
Like the dishes aren't done and the house isn't clean
But it's not that it's bothering
But that once again, she's been alone in doing everything
That she's tired, but tired doesn't always mean sleepy
Lethargic and lacking energy
She is drained
Her soul is battered and sometimes dripping in pain
But she may never say those words
Not to your face
You have to ask her, cause the burden in her will tell her what not to say
The burden in her will always say
Keep it to yourself, no one cares anyway
You ever met a woman who realizes something new about herself each and every day?
Like, why I used to hate myself?
But at the same time, isn't sure how to make that feeling go away?
Like, you're filled to the brim with insecurities and it's really unattractive
Your neediness is needing too much
You should really put a cap on it
Like, you love too hard, and I really can't stand it
But also, you love so hard, and I'm really quite proud of it
You ever met a woman who struggles with stuff that's supposed to be natural
Like love and happiness
It comes so easy, but she second guesses when she's in it
Happy gets interjected by pessimistic
And love always seems to get halted

But she can do the impossible, seemingly fine
You ever met a woman who does everything for everyone
But doesn't leave any leftover
Doesn't have the energy to give herself the leftovers
She often forgets to eat
Forgets to take care of herself and then remembers too late
that she needs someone like her too
So eventually gives herself the freedom to need some me
time too
You ever met a woman
Who can actually love without conditions?
Who can see your hurt for what it is
And connect it to your actions
Who can be patient in your healing
And help you find the right path, and
Who can, see your soul through your eyes
And hold you up when you need to cry
Because she's so understanding that she knows men have to
heal their insides
Too
Have you ever met a woman like that?
Covered in yellow caution tape
Warning everyone to step back
Because she's already deemed herself a monster
But really, she's just got some bad habits
Someone else's voice echoes and every time she believes it
She's gullible, skeptical as all hell, but every time, she
believes it
Have you ever met a woman like this?
Messy with pure intentions

Dripping with love and tasting of salvation

You ever met a woman who came with an advisory label?

I dream of it
You know
I close my eyes and my eyes wander
To worlds I never knew
If the first love I ever had is the bar or lesson not to
I close my eyes and dream of things
Like feeling safe and comfortable in someone else's arms
My heart, free of harm
I think I was put on earth to love and be loved
As my cells yearn for a warm touch
And I also think that it does not exist and will remain a myth
The duality of my heart may cause more hurt
Than the heartbreak itself
Reminding me on a daily basis that my confliction is the summation
Of moments someone else painted
In which I gained wrinkle lines from wincing at the pain, and
I dream of it, you know
To love and be loved
Or to just let go.

I read through all the books I had gotten that day, one of them was an immense letdown, while the other two were surprisingly good. Maybe, I will always blindly and distractedly choose my books from now on.

After a few weeks went by, I ran my regular errands including returning my books. I got my regular iced matcha green tea, and it was a beautiful day out. Despite the breeze blowing, I decided on a light-yellow sundress and strappy sandals.

I felt good today, the birds would also agree. Through the breeze, I could hear them whistle and chirp their songs, I didn't even need to push start on my playlist. I made my way through the doors of the library and got ready to wait in line to scan each barcode.

Next thing I know, I saw this very handsome guy again, only this time, I didn't have to wish that I was the girl in a movie, because something was happening right in front of me, at a speed so quickly that I had no idea how to process it.

Where one second, he was noticing me, now he was right in front of me. He was taller than I remembered. He seemed solid, like a man that would never waver. I'm not sure how I came to that conclusion after only seeing him twice, but seeing his demeanor in front of me, I just had this gut feeling of reassurance.

My gut had been wrong so many times before, so I didn't know why I was so supportive of it right now, but I truly just had a feeling about this one. His hand was extended, and I assumed he wanted a handshake.

I don't even know the last time a guy wanted to shake my hand, so already, I was very confused. All the thoughts racing across my brain had a matching facial expression, and this handsome guy was a getting front row to the hot mess sitcom that I was.

Then I saw him smile, he looked as nervous as I felt, which made me feel a lot better, and a lot less nervous. He had a really sweet, crooked smile. Like it took years of teenage mischief and living loudly to get that beautifully lived in. His beautiful smile made me smile, and next thing you know, neither of us were nervous.

"Hi, I'm Hazel," I said through my grin. Noah offered to buy me a coffee, and I swear, it was the best cup of coffee I have ever had in my life. The funny part is that I don't even remember the kind of coffee I got or the place we went to.

The only thing I knew was that sitting with him, drinking in his smile and sipping on something sweet—both of which were warm—made it the best cup of coffee I've ever had, because I was having it with him.

All nervous smiles aside, our conversation was fun and light. He was kind and as tough on the outside as he was, he was kind of a goof on the inside. We exchanged phone numbers and made plans for a date. My nerves came flooding in and out, like little flurries in my spine and chest.

It wasn't the regular anxieties that I'd experienced, but something light and fun. He made butterflies in my stomach that I didn't know were more than just a saying. As skeptical as I was, I was looking forward to seeing him again.

Willing

I don't remember the last time I excitedly counted how many dates I had with another person. But here we were, six amazing dates later. First was coffee, simple and sweet. Second was the park for a picnic, more intimate and in the sun.

Third was a beautiful dinner at a beautiful restaurant, in a beautiful town. Each date was more intimate than the last, yet we'd only ever touched souls, not skin. Tonight, I wanted to take Noah to the stars.

There was something about seeing how small we were in a vast place that was eerily calming to me. So, I wanted him to be calm with me. I went to high school with the manager of the observatory, so I may have asked to keep the place open after hours, for just the two of us.

It was seven-thirty that evening, I wore a simple dress with wedges, hair up in a ponytail and almost no makeup. The more time we spent together, the more I just wanted to be me, and if he continued to accept me, fresh-faced and all, then maybe this could go somewhere.

Noah was wearing dark blue jeans and a white tee, topped with an olive-green bomber jacket. His style was very put together, crisp and clean, and then lightly sprayed with a scent you'd want to embrace yourself in. *He was so handsome.*

"You look so beautiful," he said to me with a beautifully crooked smile. His eyes were a greenish blue, like an ocean, or a garden, either way I could spend all day there.

There was a small blush beginning to burn in my cheeks, so I instinctively dropped my gaze toward the floor as I gave out an involuntary chuckle. "Thank you."

We started on the exhibits that showed us the constellations that we would be able to see if the city lights took a night off. The Big Dipper, made up of 7 major stars— Ursa Major, Orion's Belt, three bright stars—Alnitak, Alnilam, and Mintaka, The Little Dipper.

"So, if you could live in the stars, what constellation would you choose to live in?" He asked me, and I had never been asked such a question, but I felt like it would be very telling of the kind of person I was, even though living among the stars in general would be amazing.

"Maybe, now hear me out," as my smile grew wider at the absurdity of what I was about to say, "I don't have to choose just one constellation, and I can just float around space from one place to the next. Kind of like a game of *pong* and I'm the little ball just bouncing around."

Laughter consumed us in the moment, and I felt myself fall into him so beautifully and so naturally. It felt good to give my laughs a home, but it felt even better when his arms accepted me and let me live in his embrace, even for just a moment.

There was a giant room that we went to next, and when you looked up, the entire ceiling was a projection of space. Every star seemed within reach, and I so badly wanted to reach out and touch them. I motioned to lie on the floor, swiping my dress beneath me to make sure nothing would have been exposed and he didn't hesitate to lie right beside me.

"I'm not so knowledgeable about space that I can point out details and facts, but it's more like a feeling. Ya know? Like, down here, on Earth, we are overwhelmed with problem after problem, trauma after trauma, and it's relentless. It doesn't seem to stop."

"So, to pull myself out of my clustered thoughts, I like to stargaze and remind myself that in the grand scheme of things, there's no problem that's bigger than this," my hands motioned upward and outward to the magnitude of the stars and space before us.

"Then it brings me back down from my heightened emotions, and it just puts things into perspective. It's calming, ya know?"

"I get that, it's like, this is so big, and we are so small, so what exactly are we freaking out over?" He concurred. "I think it's fascinating, really. Space is so vast and dense; I'd love to be able to get out and see it for myself. Really though, I'd like to meet a couple aliens, ask them how they managed survival without an atmosphere and how do I get on that. Then we could ditch Earth all together."

He chuckled as the satire slipped from his smile, and I laughed into him. This time, lying down, my bashful face slightly covered by my hands, still wanting to turn to him as I did.

Again, he let me; his laughing slowed, and he placed a very delicate finger on my chin, leaning in for a kiss. And now, kissing under the stars is my favorite place to be with him.

***

It was three hours into our date, and I swore it felt like it'd only been ten minutes. I didn't want the night to end, and Noah wasn't giving any inclination that he did either. The observatory was long behind us now, and I suggested something sweet.

"Frozen yogurt is my favorite," I told him as we walked through the park under the faded star-lit sky. The city lights forced the sky to dull but could never take away its beauty.

"You barely got any yogurt," he laughed, "that's all toppings in there, like, I see maybe a spoonful of yogurt, and the rest is cheesecake bits and strawberries."

I couldn't deny his keen observation, so all I could was say that he was absolutely right. Our laughter was the soundtrack of the evening, and I don't think I would ever change the station.

Things never felt heavy with him, and maybe that was the newness of whatever this was, but either way, I think I can speak for both of us when I say, we really just wanted to enjoy it a little bit longer.

"What do you picture in your future?" I questioned as we sat ourselves at a park bench.

"What do you mean? Relationship-wise, career-wise?" I was stuck on what I wanted to say, and he began to answer anyways, "I think that I just want moments like this, where nothing feels forced and I can be happy. In the past, I was *trying* to be happy. But I think maybe that's where it started to go bad."

"I was with this girl—I know, you're not supposed to talk about your exes, sorry—but I was with this girl, and we did everything that couples were supposed to do, but she was so content with what we were, and never tried to move forward."

"She was happy with her friends, her job, her life, and so, I needed to be happy too. I almost forced it on myself to be happy. I let go of this really great opportunity out of state because she refused to grow with me; when I continued to grow, she continued to fight it."

"Happiness, or what was supposed to be happiness, became this girl who I thought I loved, yelling all the time. I looked back and thought I was doing something all wrong, but really, I just want to be with someone who loves me enough to let me be happy and grow."

"Not someone who forces me to be happy to their standards. I didn't wanna go out anymore, the nightlife wasn't something I wanted to keep doing. I didn't want to go to pool parties or get wasted or anything like that anymore. And she made me feel like shit because I didn't want that."

"It's dumb, it's all really dumb to say out loud, but it wasn't great; it made me realize that wherever I am in the future, if I ever fell for someone again, she would allow me to be authentically happy at my level and push me to go where I wanted to in life, not hold me back."

Noah sat there, pensive, and on the verge of blushing for fear of over-sharing. Little did he know, I loved over-sharing. It was this involuntary spill of guts that helped you really get to know someone.

Kind of like the way his eyes would crinkle and wince when he seemed triggered, or the way that his natural smile was crooked. The more vulnerable we became, the less we hid our imperfections.

I found myself exhaling more with him, which was a pleasant feeling because there were no nerves at the top of my throat that forced me to inhale and wait it out.

"First of all, it's not dumb at all, that all makes perfect sense. You should have someone who loves you for you, and I think that means loving you through your stages and being accepting of the fact that one version of you isn't guaranteed forever."

"Cause that's what we're all striving for, right? Growth? I know I am. And of course, we all want someone to grow with. Sorry that you were ever made to feel like you couldn't."

I caught his red cheeks before he looked into his frozen yogurt cup, he nodded in agreement and said, "What about you?"

"I think for me," it was harder to get the words out when it was about myself. "I just want a partner. I don't think I have ever experienced that before, but someone to do life with. Build with, grow with, love with, smile with, and cry with.

"I want the hard stuff to be just as acceptable as the good because at the end of the day, we're a team. At the end of the day, whatever the problem is, we'll fix it together. Ya know? I want unshakable trust, unshakable love, just unshakable."

"I'm not sure how real that is, but that's what I want. Then *we* can choose how our life will play out. *We* can choose where, and *we* can choose when. I don't know where I will see my work in a few years, or anything like that. But if there is someone by my side at that point, maybe we just figure it all out together."

***

I want a terribly ugly love. Because I think more often than not, I'm not the prettiest. And I want a love that accepts me that way, or not at all. I want the midnight cravings and the morning after guilt for indulging in a sweet that was far too sweet and not worth it. But doing it again the next day.

I want to witness the panics and be dressed for battle just in case you need help attacking back. I want the doubts to flood from your lips until you've exhausted all the possible scenarios of how I may break your heart, and then I want to hold each other until midnight strikes.

We can laugh over a shared, regrettable meal. The doubts melt together until we can't even taste them, and we indulge until the sun decides to wake and check on us. I want fears to leak from your eyes until there's none left, because your throat chakra is finally so free and clear that you have no problem speaking.

Our fears can mingle and get to know each other, fade away into the mist and live happily ever after. What's next? What else can we messily exhaust from our bodies together. Each ugly event after another brings us closer, making us one.

I want the *ugly love*, the *break down old habits love*, the *reduce my trauma responses to none* kind of love, the *open and honest conversations that have been trapped on the tip of my tongue* kind of love, the *I'm scared, but I'd try for you* kind of love, the kind of love that makes me listen to terribly ugly beautiful songs and want to dance and sing all night long - even though, I can't carry a tune.

I want the ugly stuff. Because somehow, in a scientific way, or a spiritual, religious, metaphorical, actual way... it makes for a beauty that no one could ever fabricate. No one can reduce, no one can take.

There's a willingness in my bones
And it felt good
Like a home
Or a rocking chair on a porch
It felt like basking in the sunrise
Morning birds singing songs
And I, lids closed, humming along
The willingness leaped into my heart
I went from a warm flutter
To a cold stop
But the flooding kept flooding my aortic chambers
One by one, like fantasizing over one day children
It was you I named them after
Willingness in my left ventricle
Circulating through my body
And my blood, from red
Turned the color of daisies
I'm a garden
And you're the sun
I'm blooming
Because, by the grace of willingness itself
I think I may have found the one
Willingness becomes me
Down to my humbled bones

Willingness becomes me
And I have found a home.

I want to get to know you deep down and personal
I want to know where you go when your eyes fall blank, and
your mind's gone lost
And what do I need to do to help you get found again
Is coming home easy for you
Or do you struggle to find the familiar walls of safety and
comfort
Forgetting that they hold truth
Forgetting that those walls hold much of you
I know your favorite color is green, like the trees that bustle
in the wind
And your favorite food is anything warm
You look down when you walk
And your favorite jeans are torn
But I also know that scary movies are less scary when
you're not alone
And sometimes, you ache in your shoulders
And you're always ready for an adventure even when you
yawn
I know you love really hard, even though you've learned a
lesson or some
But your optimism is beyond anything I've ever touched
And I want to know where you get the strength to shake
things off

I want to know your bad days the way I get to enjoy your
good
Because you're always there for them
Now, I think it's time for you to have someone.

Teach me what the word beautiful means
Sunday school and I am anew
Read me psalms as I hold onto your palms
Heaven-sent waterfalls that water your cheeks
Bloom rose red petals when you smile or when you weep
Loving me until every petal falls mercilessly
Beauty in the way your eyes meet mine
Looking beneath the curtains to take a peek into my mind
Windows to the soul
And you hold the view
So, this beauty you behold
Chocolate with tints of gold
Dark rimmed eyes lined with eyelashes for days
Wings on the forefront of miracles that fly me away
Get lost in your brown golden honey, nights that make me
want to stay
Trusting eyes that keep my secrets safe
Caring eyes that wish my wishes and pray
Weathered hands that fought through storms
Bruised knuckles, red and worn
Beauty in your protective hands
The way they are so hardened, but I've never felt more
gentle hands
They are so big; how do you carry the entire world like that

Beauty in your gracious stride
Arms swinging and offering help to those around
Give a giving hand
Teach me beauty like that.

She was different than anyone you may have ever met, so be careful. Not because she was fragile or dainty. Not because she was one to watch out for. Not because she needed the extra help—because she didn't.

She was a goddamned force and you had never seen a woman like her. Resiliency was her mother, and she was spoon-fed strength. She had rebuilt her life more times than one person should ever have to.

She had experienced loss in unthinkable ways. She had come face to face with demons three times her size. That woman was less human than anyone I'd ever seen. She made godly seem like an understatement.

But when you meet her, you will get the idea that she wasn't even aware of her own power. You'd see the humbled angel that she is because she exuded it from her radiant skin in the yellow aura that she possessed.

She'd been through hell and back and her tough, yet supple skin had never been pierced. Her heart was still gold, and she was still pure today as she was before life made a mess of her soul.

For someone as bright as she is, you'd never know that she had army-crawled her way through the black, white and every square inch of gray area that life had to offer her. Only someone who had seen as much dark as she had, could ever be that bright. *And she is bright.*

She is the sun peaking over the mountaintops; the break of dawn when the air is crisp and solid. The dew that kissed the tops of leaves and the hum of the birds early in the morning, still alive and beautiful because people hadn't disturbed the streets yet.

She is that moment. Bright and early, only a few will get to appreciate that, and still, they'd pass her by. But if you ever get to her, if you ever get to breathe in the crisp morning air and see how whole and beautiful and all-encompassing, she is—don't pass her by.

You'd miss her and you won't get a chance like that again. Unlike the sunrise, she doesn't come around every day. So, when you see her, try to think to yourself your intentions, because if you just want to bottle up her light and steal it for yourself, then keep going. She has had more than enough people steal away at her—*and still, she is bright.*

And don't get me started on the way she knows how to love; that woman is all heart. If love were something we had to learn, then she was the teacher. I'm convinced that she created it, shaped it, gave it red-hot blood, and whispered to it, "Kiss everyone in the world."

She's selfless that way. She created love when she spoke, and she was always sure to speak it outward. Every time she ever felt over the moon happy, she shared it with whoever she was with, as if it were the last slice of her favorite cake. With hungry and wide eyes, she will still give it to you.

Her laugh is full-bodied, each decibel bounced off the walls and decorated the room with joy. Have you ever met anyone who could do that? Her laugh made you feel love. Her nose crinkled and her eyes wrinkled, and she hid her smile when she did it, but you still can't help but see how beautiful her smile really is. Her laugh made you feel something, anything, *everything*. She was an anomaly, that woman.

She was a walking contradiction—a lover and a fighter. She was an ocean of love, and though her waves crashed, and she may roar, she knew no conflict. The very act of it didn't exist within her abilities.

She could crush ships and drown the worst of them, but as naturally as the tide rose and currents pulled, she would only gently sway and push. In the same breath, she would go to war for someone she loved.

She had fought through adversity to stay afloat, fighting through a storm of tears to smile, she had broken barriers within her mind to expand from the confines that she once placed within and continuously elevated into new levels of personal growth.

There were no limits that could stop a warrior like her. And for those she loved, she was even more relentless. Even more daring to persist.

Though she never slept well, she was a lullaby. Being with her was like having peaceful, soothing nights. A full moon and dimmed city lights, you would see every star in the sky. She's like being able to sit cliffside and see them all for the first time.

She's the moment you marvel at falling stars and wishes made. That type of peace and joy that combats anxiety and slowed your heart to a steady, strong beat. She's a compilation of those moments.

Climbing in a bed of freshly dressed sheets after a warm shower. She's chamomile tea and a splash of honey.

I just never fathomed a person, who's less person
More of a figment of my imagination
A mirage in the landscape of barren land
A delusion that I dreamed up one day, and ever since tried
so hard to trip like that again
A dream
I just never fathomed that a dream of a person
Could exist, here in person
And it wasn't that this dream was perfect
Quite the opposite, in fact
Imperfection draped her canvas like velvet curtains
And it was the most beautiful display of art I'd ever seen
The way that pessimism insisted on living through this living being
The way that skepticism insisted on being heard and seen
The way that closed minded held tight to old locks and never gave way to newer things
Imperfect was the tone
For which this dream of a being was colored
But transparent enough to where I could see where the love was under key.

You would never know that she'd been through the things that she had. She carried herself with such a grace that she made you feel gracious by association. Her hair was long, thick and wild.

Curl clumps hung like vines and framed her face. It was right on the cusp of brown and black. Inside, when she sat beside me on the couch, it looked dark, like results of mixing her favorite cake batter. But when she stepped outside, her hair became this gorgeous rich brown, as if the sun had lent her its rays to shine.

And her eyes were even more magnificent. The color of forgiveness and home. You could get lost in her gray-brown irises, but here was the kicker, you'd find that you were never in a rush to get found. She was magnificent.

When she stretched to the tips of her toes to reach the top shelf and still managed to struggle, she never asked for help. She would climb countertops like it was an Olympic sport and always win.

Her 5'2" frame fit perfectly in my arms, almost as if she was made for me—scientifically proven by the way her head was level with my chest.

For someone who embodied a lot of light, a lot of sun-kissed and bright, she wore a modern look. The neutral tones complimented the golden-brown honey in her skin.

I could really talk about Hazel every day. But I'd rather spend my moments getting lost in her. Her mind was even more alluring. She had this deep connection between her heart and mind, able to empathize and truly understand—all at once.

Where it took me time to even care a little bit for others, she tried first and foremost to see through their eyes. Passing out the benefit of the doubt like it was her civil duty. People were better off after knowing her, I know I am.

"You're really beautiful, know that?"

His voice was scruffy, rough even. Like he'd smoked a pack of cigarettes each day for a decade, though I don't think he'd ever touched the stuff.

"You're a liar." It was a bad habit of mine to never accept a compliment. I was never taught that they were mine to accept. I was never made to feel that I was allowed to own such a thing as beauty.

Blood rushed through my cheeks, and I instinctively looked away. I couldn't meet his garden eyes any longer without getting lost in the sun. How embarrassing; to fall so senselessly for this man and yet here I was, fallen. I hoped he could never tell how willfully in love with him I was.

He reached his fingers out in such a delicate way, cradled my chin in his fingertips and brought my gaze back to his beautiful eyes. It felt good to be so close to him. I felt like the outside world was muted and I didn't have to worry about anything.

I wouldn't say safe was the feeling I felt, but I was teetering on the brink of it—as close as I'd ever fucking been to feeling safe with someone—and any moment now, I'd happily fall.

"Don't do that," his baritone voice paused, and he started again with intensity, "don't shy away. You're fucking beautiful, you took my breath away the moment I saw you at the library. You had your head down though, so your hair fell past your cheeks, and I felt like I lost it because something that beautiful shouldn't be hidden. I lost all sense of time; nothing made sense anymore. But then I saw you again, and time started again. I had to tell you, because you're really fucking beautiful."

My eyes watered in disbelief, and he wiped my tears as they reluctantly fell down my cheeks. And then it happened. I wasn't on the brink anymore. With my cheek resting in his palm, as if it had been looking for a place to call home and finally stumbled upon it, I felt safe. And I fell into it.

I fell into him; not because he called me beautiful. Not because he saw me when I couldn't see myself. But because he saw through me, into the depths of my chest. Because he was delicate and warm in a harsh and cold world. Because he was everything I had never experienced, a needed and cherished change of pace.

I want you to give me hope
In ways so big that I am blinded and at the same time, I have
never seen more
Blindly falling to depths that I am happy to fall
Knowing damn well if I break and bleed, it was worth the
fall
Knowing if you don't catch me, the fall was worth it all
Because falling into you
And on to you
Catch on to your hand and seeing my palm find a home in
yours
My head finally have a place to rest
Falling meant feeling safe at last
All of those delicate details that paint the picture of us
Was worth it in the end
Even if the painting gets sold in the end
Loving you was art
And I was honored to be half the muse and play that part
Symphonic melodies danced around my ears
Every time your thumbs brushed my hair
It was very much worth it in the end
Hope filled enough that even though I knew it wouldn't last
I never suspected an end until I got there and all I could do
was sit there and laugh

I could only laugh and smile because for a moment in time
I got to love to my heart's content.

There ought to be bull in my blood
Because I know it's in my skull
Bull-headed, my mother used to call me
And I know it was so by every time I would refuse that title
with my fists at my side
Stomping a foot with all too much pride
I felt like that now, teetering on the line
Where something that resembles love resides
It's talking to me, asking for me to release any ill-colored
reservations
But I, a stubborn woman
Have nothing but patience
I could sit all day, weighing the pros and cons of giving my
heart away
Maybe I just do it different this time
Making sure I take my time, presently and transparent
Maybe I just walk slow
Allow my heart and mind to move at the same pace, never
letting one get ahead cause it's not a race
Maybe I just walk in a different woman than last time
A little more present
A little less trusting
A little more willing
A little more loving.

They say I should be weak
Let a man come to meet me in my time of need
with a heart full of strings
that only I can pull
Playing chords like a harp
Plucking away, my melody the siren song
And love follows shortly after, but never too long
Weaken at the knees, so someone can finally see eye to eye
with me
But I can't do that, you see?
My other half could never meet me in a time of *weak*
Because he should either reciprocate or exceed me
He should equal me, or teach me
I would never find my love, my sweet and strong love
Beneath me
I could never live there, that's a place you'd never meet me.

You make me brave
You make me bold
You make me want to walk straight up to you
Look you right in the face
Strong enough not to melt into your gaze
With two soft fingers
And a brush of your lip
Take that cigarette
And bump the tip
Ash falls to the floor
As I taste the nicotine right from your kiss
You make me bold enough to want to inhale your poison
Addicted to the bite and sting that comes with a deep inhale
I breathe you in, but you don't feel wrong
You feel like soothing vapor caressing my tongue
Like healing smoke that heals my lungs
I breathe you in, and brave I've become
Daring to try new things, each and every day
With one caveat, I'm afraid
I only want to try them at the tips of your fingers
While we're linked at the wrists
I want to experience new moments
Entirely with you
Because you make me bold, brave, and daring too.

He doesn't just hear me, he listens
And he doesn't just see me
He takes long pauses to gaze
See if there are any contortions in the shape of my face
He checks for furrowed brows or sunken eyes
He doesn't just feel my skin
He holds me until his is mine
And our space is fused together
And we get to unwind
I don't just taste his lips
I crave his kiss.

Struggling to make sense of you

Mentally invested in my desire to kiss you

Invested in your eyes

Exhaling kisses into your smile

I am struggling to make sure thinking of you doesn't become a habit

But then again

There are worse things to be addicted to.

I find myself lusting him
With the cool morning breeze that floats through my
window at 5am
With the sun setting on the beach and our toes in the sand
With his eyes locked on me
When he thought I was asleep
But I seen him, see me
And I saw his look taking me in
Like a deep inhale
But this wind went straight to his heart
I find myself lusting him
But the more stolen glances I find him in
The more times we lust
I learn we don't just fuck
We are making history
With this chemistry
It's a project originated in the stars
Now here on earth
In the most wonderful timing
This lusting feels like a deeper something
And I know that this was meant to be ours
So, I find myself lusting his essence
So, I can take in his presence
So, I can love on his effort

And make chemistry in his bedroom
And the stars knew it all along
So, here I am
Feeling like I found a pair of arms in which I belong.

Could I even surrender?
With a heart glued back together with intentions and prayer
Could I ever bring myself to surrender?
To let go and trust someone with my heart—beating, but
still tender
Could I ever even surrender?
After all the fires I put out to find me again
Could I ever give that up?
Or put it all beside me
Do I have to surrender to fall in love?
To give in to the cravings for someone else's touch
Do I have to surrender?
Just to spend some time with someone else
Can I still have my makeshift heart, all to myself?
Can both realities be true?
Where I can start to fall in love
But still have all of me, too?
What does it even mean to surrender?
In regard to love, my heart and someone new?

Want to know what I'm craving?
A kiss so deep that I worry I may be addicted to it
One so raw that the rest of the world ceases to exist
And I begin to forget everything
For the moments that I am entranced
By lips like liquid courage
And with a kiss like that
I could be courageous enough
To want everything that follows
The steam filled moments that keep me lost
The rough touch that somehow feels soft
The blankets crumpling and falling to the floor
The pushing and pulling
The praying for more.

It was about 86 degrees that evening, the fans didn't seem to be blowing out cold enough air and all the energy was exhausted from our bodies. Noah and I lay on the bed as stretched out as we can possibly be, even being right beside me, I wished we were closer, but the heat was making physical contact a foreign concept.

So, we lay there, I was stripped down to my underwear and tank top while he was just wearing shorts. There was nothing on TV worth watching, but we didn't care much.

"Okay," he said, "my turn," as we asked the 33rd question in our game of 21 Questions. "How do you picture your dream home?"

"Oh, that's a good one!" My fingers reached out for his as I shifted around in the bed. "I've never actually put too much thought into the whole thing, but I guess, the things I look forward to the most are," I pondered on what felt like a heavy question.

"I want to be able to sit on the patio, in a rocking chair and drink my morning coffee. And when I want to retreat, I want books everywhere. Well, maybe not everywhere." I giggled at the absurdity.

"I want an office with books along the walls, just like West Peak. A big comfy chair in there and all kinds of books. I think a big yard would be nice because eventually we'll get a dog. *Hmm,* maybe a nice big kitchen so we can have big family meals. I think that's it. Those are the things that I picture when I think of my home one day." I smile with distinction because I know that was a thorough answer. "Oh! And a lot of fruit trees in the yard!"

I'm not even sure she realizes that she said we *so many times, but I hope in her mind, in her dreams of her home, when she says* we, *that I'm there.*

"I love it," Noah responds with a smile, "count me in. Okay, your turn now."

I contemplated my next question carefully, "do you ever picture kids and marriage in your future?" That felt like a loaded question, but we were being so open and vulnerable, I felt it okay to ask anyways.

"Oh definitely. I want kids, and I want a family. My dad and mom were never together, so I don't know what that looks like, but I do know what I want. Like, I want all of our friends there, everyone we love. I want my mom there to see her son being the good man she raised about to be an even better man by marrying the love of his life."

"I think I want to write my own vows, too. Cause I think it'll be personal that way, more heartfelt, ya know? And then I just picture the most beautiful woman walking toward me in a long white dress."

He caressed my cheek as he began, "I know she's got these dark, gorgeous eyes, beautiful smile, and thick, curly hair." I couldn't help but interrupt his future vision and kissed him in the middle of his sentence.

"And then, we're gonna party our asses off with all the people we love, and it'll be the best night of our lives. Then, we'll have some babies and life will be good. Yeah, I've thought about it. One day, it'll happen."

"I didn't realize you put so much thought into it! I like it, it sounds beautiful." I couldn't help but smile. As we painted the picture of what we both expected our futures to look like, the painting grew more and more similar with every question.

Garden wedding. Two dogs running around the yard. Two or three children, two boys and one girl or one of each. We would want our house in a place that was not too deep in the city, but also not so far from everyone else.

Family vacations at least once a year and a promise to always make sure that we were reminded of coming back to each other despite the stress of life. Wherever our one-day, maybe would be, our home would be the place we come to for peace and to be able to shed all the weight of the world once we walked through the door.

I didn't want to put too much pressure on the thought of whether our future would become as beautiful as we described. I just wanted to live in the moment for as long as I could, and if we were lucky enough to live it one day, then I would be happy.

***

I woke up at 2:30 in the morning, unsure if I fell asleep mid-question or if he did. As quietly as I could, I got off the bed and tiptoed my way into the kitchen. The temperature had cooled enough to be able to function, and as parched as I was, I needed to get a glass of water.

I let my memory of the apartment guide me through the dark as I made my way into the kitchen. The light from the refrigerator illuminated the area as I stood in the cool of it, sipping water.

Behind me, an awakened Noah came and wrapped his arms around me. My eyes closed instinctively and gently, knowing that in his arms is the safest place I'd ever have the chance to exist.

His warmth was the perfect balance with the cool of the fridge. He didn't say a word, only kissed me gently on the neck, and again on the cheek. The strap on my tank top slid off my shoulder and he caressed my arm with a delicate finger, lifting the strap until it returned to its place.

Not sure how I got here, not sure how I felt so relaxed, and not sure where we went from here. But I was a willing passenger with him. I was willing to try new things, willing to explore love without the fear of consequences, and willing to be present in every moment shared.

We stood silently for a moment more. The cup of water was now set on the counter and me, now turned around facing Noah's heart—its beating was the soundtrack of this embrace.

I imagine moments like this that all added up and will one day leave me so full that the words *I love you* spilled from my lips and if we were lucky enough to live it one day, then I would be happy.

But for now, we retreated to the now cooled bed. I lay on his chest and listened to his heartbeat lull me to sleep.

I get it
To surrender to a love
And all its possibilities
To give in to the ebb and flow that somehow amounts to
more than just my needs
To live so presently in the moment that I forget the walls
that I once built around me
I get to be one with the foundation that we've built
And find balance in each other, when the world is at a tilt
I'm learning I don't lose me to love you
I'm learning that surrendering isn't painful
I'm learning that I'm still me and I'm still here
I'm still whole, but now I get to have you
The painting of the love we will one day make is a beautiful
view
I'm learning that in order to see it, I need to surrender a little
bit too.

Refreshing

You ever wonder why the darkest hour is the most pure
How thoughts become tangible, and hearts beat out your
chest and the pounding is all you hear
Each night I fall until I can't fall anymore
Then the next, I'm proven wrong, and I never stop fallin'
Cause at 2am, when the world is dark
And the outside noises are dimmed down to nothing, I feel
everything
Every nerve ending is exposed
And I learn that's why they call it intimate
Just you and me, feeling everything all at once
Every heartbeat, beats with purpose
Every word, exhaled with honesty when it's spoken
It's too late at night to put your vulnerabilities aside
Too late to not address our fears
And too late to put up facades and only present the prettiest
parts of ourselves
It's why I love 2am
With you, it's never tiring
Never wondering, why are we awake at this hour?
It's become the best part of my weeks

Waking up to moments that only you and I can make
2am is a feeling that only you and I could create.

Sometimes, I let myself get carried away in what ifs and
maybes
In love stories that mildly exist
And your hand resting on my stomach
Saying hello to our one-day baby
Sometimes, I let myself dream up tomorrow and one-days
Where we're driving down the road
Playing music, feeling sun rays
Otis Redding on the radio
'I've been loving you' sound waves
Sometimes, I imagine a plausible future
That's too far stretched and impossible
But feels like second nature
And feels like what I could wake up to tomorrow
Wrapped around your torso
Warm and secured
Feeling love through the sweatshirt that I sometimes steal
to wear
Feeling safety in your arms
And home in your sing along songs
Hearing the cracks in your voice
And sharing covers until dawn
Sometimes, I lie awake and crave a kiss I never knew
Crave a touch I never felt

Crave a *you* kind of view
Sometimes, when I'm driving and hear the music playing
I let myself dream and love where it takes me
Then I feel reality shake me
And my fears start to break me
And my walls begin to encase me
And sometimes turns back into maybe
But I hope that sometimes creeps up and distracts me
Because sometimes, is actually really sweet.

Today was different. I knew Noah to be an amazing and kind person. Maybe I saw too much of his kindness and less of his humanness. Because he was very much human; raw and ridden with emotions, and I must have looked past it.

Just as I had my ups and downs, so did he. And I could have run, I could have drawn a line right then and there, because he introduced me to the side of him that was patient and sweet. I could have walked away because I wasn't inclined, nor obligated to deal with the shortcomings and short-handed emotions he was presenting.

He gave me the impression that not an angry cell lived in his bones, and yet, here he was. He was so fucking angry, and I expected him to yell. History taught me that this was the turning point where he stopped being the way he was in the beginning.

He would probably stop telling me why he loved me and let me know that my flaws were too much. So, I waited for him to yell at me, at the walls, at the vodka, at the world. Even though I didn't do anything, I was just waiting for him to scream.

But he never did, not at me, nor the walls and it dawned on me that this anger didn't have a root cause of anything other than life is frustrating. Instinctually, I assumed it was me, but that wasn't the case.

Today must have been one thing after another. He didn't drink his anger away. By the day's end, there were no holes punched through the wall and he never looked at me like he wanted nothing to do with me.

His eyes never suggested that everything was my fault. And his voice never got carried away as the sound came toward me.

This was one day, in particular, where I felt my walls come down a little bit more. I initially felt closed off to him because of the impending battle that never came, but I ended up feeling a sense of protection for him.

I think I loved this man, even when he was boiling. I was scared at first, but he managed to reassure me that there was nothing to fear here. *And there wasn't.* Then, at the end of the day, after his anger subsided, he wrapped his arms around me and exhaled.

He was just a human, with very human emotions. Sometimes, I too boiled over and couldn't think straight. In those moments, I would only ever want the benefit of doubt and a loving shoulder.

So often, men never get to be emotional—they never get to showcase fear, overwhelming stress or sadness, or frustration. But if I was to ask Noah to love me in all of my human emotions, then I would always make sure he could do the same.

I would always make sure that I provided the same safety he gave me. So, rather than walking in the face of a vulnerable and new fear, I stayed and gave him the love I would have wanted.

Life got on top of him, and it came out in floods and waves. And I decided that that was okay. He wasn't malicious in any way as he felt these things, he was only human and deserved a lot of grace.

I had to learn to stop thinking through a past lens because Noah had never done anything to suggest he was the same. Noah deserved every single benefit of the doubt that I had left to distribute.

He'd been patient with me when I was at my worst, he'd been kind when I needed understanding. He'd been perfect when I'd been a mess. My gut agreed with me.

***

Today was a fucking shit show, sometimes you just wake up and it seems like everything is out to get you. It didn't seem like anything went right, and all I could do was let it fucking happen.

Nothing monumental, but little things here and there that built up. Stacked, one on top of the other, so it seemed like a mountain of headaches by the end of the day. I could feel Hazel distancing from me, and I knew that my anger wasn't her burden, so I let her.

I dealt with it on my own, I didn't shove it down, but solved my fucking shit and let it die down, knowing damn well that something could make everything better. Knowing damn well that her smile could solve every problem.

Her scent, eucalyptus and limes, was the aromatherapy that could heal everything. I knew that holding her in my arms would slow my heart down from a high rage to a steady calm; so, by the end of the day I did that. I held her and breathed her in.

At this stage, I knew I loved this woman beyond any depth I ever knew I could love someone else, only she didn't know it yet. She was where I had found peace in the world and I didn't really know how to voice that to her just yet, but she was refreshing.

One day, I would work up the nerve to tell her that, but I didn't want to scare her off with too serious or too deep of emotions. If only she knew, her existence would make mine worth it.

"I'm sorry about how I was today, you didn't deserve that, and I'll try to make sure you don't have to deal with that ever again," I said as I held her.

"Why are you telling me that?" Hazel questioned.

"What do you mean? I was a dick all day, I shut you out and you didn't do anything to me to deserve that. I'm sorry." Still standing behind her, with my arms wrapped around Hazel, I felt her turning so she could face me.

I instantly felt embarrassed having to look her in the eyes after how I acted today. I felt childish and immature, I felt irrational mostly. And I had to look at her, with all her grace.

"The only thing I wish that happened different," she said in the softest voice ever, like I was being draped in her velvet, "was that you let me help you when you're angry or sad, or hurt, for that matter."

She placed both of her palms on either side of my face, and I felt my eyes close while listening to her voice. "I'm here for you, Noah. I know you're going to have bad days, and I want to be a part of those too. I want you to know that you can come to me, and I'll always have my arms open for you. If there's a problem, I want to help you fix it. If you're hurt, I want to heal you. But I can't do that if you don't let me, I can't do that if you shut me out."

I felt so weakened and humbled by her words, but I also had never felt stronger. As a man, I felt like I had to constantly keep it together and be strong, but she gave me a place where I can be vulnerable, too. She allowed me to be imperfect without judgment.

I held her for as long as I could. This time, it was me who needed to be in her arms and her warmth. We stood there, in each other's safety, for minutes before I finally pulled my head back to look at her in her beautiful brown eyes.

"Thank you." I kissed her and hoped that she could feel my appreciation for her in my life. I hoped that she could feel my gratitude and intentions to never take her for granted.

I hoped she knew that I would always be there for her and would always do my best to support her the way she needed. I felt her lips pressing back to let me know that she felt the same too, and that she wasn't going anywhere either.

By the end of the day, and after being healed by Hazel, I didn't know why I was mad. The day had long since escaped me and I just wanted to be here with my one-day wife.

Every single time I was able to hold her and take her in, I was always reminded of how badly I wanted to marry her. I wanted this for the rest of my life.

The scent of eucalyptus and cashmere hangs in the air
Lingering and carrying from the tips of her hair
And when we collide
Clumsily falling into each other's lives
The crash provides an ethereal escape
In which I get to taste a little bit of her angelic grace
Humble intentions stitch together her fateful imperfections
Proving time and time again
That there is beauty in pain
When she smiles in that way
Like if the smile painted on her face
Was a holy escape
With flower petals at her feet
Her eyes whisper forget me not
And for just one second
I am floating 4 inches above ground
And the rotation of the earth stops
The smell of eucalyptus brings me home
This woman, beautifully, makes me come undone.

Since 24 hours in a day is all we have
I continuously calculate how to best make the most of it
Because I'd never knowingly waste a second that I could
spend loving you
Feasting in your eyes as we sit across the table, indulging in
a shared meal, I find myself with only 19 hours left
Choosing how to better drink in the moments
An hour under the sun, so I can remember how your skin
soaks in the rays
You can't see stars during the day
But I'm looking at my Polaris
Home, I could spend another 9 here
Balancing the hours between your singing and us sleeping
Both of which are a melody that I rest my ear on
Without even trying, 3 go by and in this time
I learn the facets of you
Never a dull moment, the kaleidoscope keeps turning and
the colors of you shine
I see you act in service of your dreams
A painter of a future that's beautiful and within reach
You give it your patience
And it's as if another 3 has slipped by
And when the sun is getting restless, deciding when to wake
again

Your sigh is the sign of exasperation
And we dissect the built-up days that have led you to this
point
I learn you through and through and through
So much so, that it feels like we're no longer two
That's it, just 1 left
And with all 3,600 seconds remaining, I familiarize my lips
with yours
Because some things just don't need to be said.

I sink further into your warmth
Like it's the heat that I need to circulate around me
The warmth that caresses my skin and relaxes me
Waking up to the sunshine and you
Waking up to the warmth of you
I lie on your side of the bed when you dress
Closing my eyes
Cause I feel safe and without stress
You cause a spring sunny day, light breeze in my chest
I haven't known distress since I locked in on your kiss
And I think that maybe this
Is all the reason I experienced life the way I did
So I try my best to question less
Cause you ain't let me down yet
So maybe, I let myself fall
And I can watch you fall too
I'm learning to fall back from all the skepticism that comes
naturally to my head
From all the years, I was cold
You got me melting too
And I'm so happy that I get to melt into you.

Is it okay
If the picture I hung of you in my mind
Is so big that words follow it around?
I'm no artist
But if there were ever a muse, you would play the part
And for once
Mind and heart
Are on the same page
Same line
Same syllable
Same start
Is it okay
That I write you into art?

I like a long kiss goodnight
Words left hanging in the air
The rendezvous between me and you
Nothing short of immaculate
No misconception
I inhaled your exhale
Regained life up on your pedestal
So, I like a long kiss goodnight
Bite your lip
And punctuate the words with my tongue
Dot dot dot
Aching to finish my thought
But I'll invite you back for more
A cohesive project, my favorite, thus far.

I made the greatest mistake I could
I fell in love with a maybe or a would
I fell in love with an idea
A might
A really, really should
I fell in love with soft embers
When life felt like hardwood
I fell in love with dreams
The fire before the soot
I made the greatest mistake I've made all year
I played the sounds of your song
And let them dance around my ear
Whirlwind of feelings around me
Deep-sea kisses, astounding
I made the greatest mistake I've made all year
Choosing it again and again
Living freely in fear.

To experience the waves that you and I will make makes me
the luckiest woman in the world
I get to bite your lip and kiss your strength, giggle with you
as the nighttime remains
Combined, we strengthen our embrace
Words at the tip of my tongue but as clear as life has gotten,
in this moment, I can't think straight
Your hands heat the back of my neck, firm, but ever so
gentle
Not commanding but asking if I'd join in the evening's tides
My kiss answers yes, mouth gasping, open wide
Now, it's just the bed, not yours or my side
We are one, joined together by passion and heaven-sent
cries
None of this is wrong, I don't even doubt it, being with you
in this way must have been a purpose in my life
The two of us swaying back and forth
Gently loving life
Losing track of time
Here on this bed,
We're stuck on island time.

Intricately fitting over the suede of your skin
Hugging the curves of your collar bone
And framing your chest
I believe your arms are the place I was meant to live in
Delicately placed around your torso and hips
I wish to be yours
Like lace fits your body
Smoothing over you
And creating a beautiful image
I firmly believe that on the day heaven calls to me
You will be my welcoming view
My angel at the gates extending a hand to greet me, too
So here on this earth
I want to love you till my dying day
Making every minute count
Until I stand before those pearly gates
You're an angel
Blessing these grounds with your light and your holy
And your voice a beautiful sound
With your intimidating beauty
A work of art
And I a fool, wishing we'd never part.

I say I miss you
And I love to hear it so
I say I miss you in moments quiet
Because I feel so inclined to bare my soul
To let you know
That since I met you
I'm at a loss for words
They don't come as easy
Because there are no questions to blurt
I don't have thoughts that hurt
I don't second guess your words
And I miss you
Even if you've just placed your lips to mine
I miss you
As soon as you walk about the door
And hug me once more
One more kiss before you have to leave and return to your
world
I miss you
Words that could very well mean
Something very different
More profound
More seen
But until that day, until my voice is planning to say

Three more words
That are permanent and certain
Then I miss you
And I love to hear it so.

I don't even know how to not feel deeply for this man that now feels like home. In nights that I can't sleep, I toss and hope to turn to the sight of him, to the warmth of him. And when he's finally within arm's reach, I don't want to sleep at all. I want to fall into his laughter until I come about his pillowy, soft voice.

This must be what happiness feels like. To laugh and joke with you long after the sun has set and said its good night wishes to the stars. Laughter is only broken by kisses; cold is completely broken by warmth. And everything is colored in gold hues. Happiness and home.

I'm so glad I met you, so glad I get to have you, to know you and be held by you. So, as we laugh and play, I fall deeper and deeper. And I don't even need to ask if that's okay. My heart and mind are, for once, on the same page.

And it's titled the exact same thing as your name.

Can I love you forever?

Can I love you when the sun sets?

When the month has been long, and we can't bear another storm

Can I love you on Tuesdays and Wednesdays and Sundays galore?

Can I reach for your hand when I'm scared?

Can I reach for your chest when the day is done and I'm tired and the tiredness has won?

Can I fall into your lips and get lost in your never-ending kiss?

Can I hold you forever and never stop?

Can I get lost in your handsome, dark thoughts?

Can I love you until the sun shines at our window and the birds chirp and the clouds part and go?

Can I love you over a meal where in between bites and sips of lemonade we laugh and talk and smile at word play?

Can I love you without my tears getting in the way?

Cause you make my eyes swell with affection, not pain tears

But love tears, so grateful I get to have you tears

Grateful I get to love you tears

Grateful to be the carrier of your demons and fears

Can I lie my head in your lap while you play with my hair till my eyelids get heavy and spine begins to settle

And we rest under the moon
The same moon that we watched when we were miles apart
The same moon that pulls tides to shores
Can I love you that long?
Can I love you to the soundtrack of beautiful soulful songs?

The biggest thing I'd learned, in getting to know Noah, was that I needed to shed all expectations of what love was supposed to be, or even what a relationship was supposed to be. I had a picture in my mind, because for some reason, I thought I knew what it all was supposed to look like.

I could recall love from my memory so vividly, having known its scent, taste, and touch, all because I owned it once. But if anything, that clouded my memory. Holding on to this idea of love, only made me see it now through a lens of judgment and expectations.

I needed to commit to living in the moment with him if I ever wanted us to have a real base to stand on. I needed to allow myself to be present and whole. I stopped letting myself overthink what could be, what if, and why.

It was then that I started to experience him and us. This allowed me to see very clearly who he was and who I was when I was with him.

Love isn't one moment or feeling

It can't be attached to one being or one night

Because it's a series of moments and on the scale that it resides

Love is the lows I find myself in, and the way I'm received in that moment

Love is when you're cared for while in pain

Love is the laughter in the mundane

Love is found in the selfless acts that add up, amounting to grace

Its fireworks, but also the calm after the burst

Love is in the way we ask, how is your mom today, do you need anything, are you hurt?

It can be in plates of food

Or a morning routine

Love is all-encompassing

Ever changing

Growing in its strides

Love can't be defined

Because it's hard to pinpoint something that makes you feel grounded, yet flying.

You're like waking up again
The way refreshed feels
I didn't know I needed you
The agony my heart felt
The pit in my stomach that wouldn't quit
The ache I held in the pocket behind my shoulder blade and
could never rub out
I could never reach the relief in which I'd seek
But if I was ever so lucky
To rest long enough
Sleep deep into dream filled voids
And let my body hang heavy
Pushing deep into my memory foam mattress
Into the crevice of you
Into the memory of you
Into the memory of your kiss
Remembering the warmth
The fire you set at my ribs
I didn't know I needed it
Then the sun leaks through my windows
And rested is a feeling I only dreamed real
But rested and relaxed, by your side, is how I feel
And then relief fills me because I look over and see that
you're real.

Here on my couch, a nothing special place
Where nothing special has happened more often than not
You looked at me
You kissed me so deep I could taste your intentions
Never wanting to jump the gun
I kiss you back to stop myself from saying anything that
would make you run
But you paused anyways
Looked me in my wide eyes
Said three words and had me paralyzed
Tears of disbelief, fear and solace fell from my eyes
You kissed them away
You kissed them into smiles
You told me that your love was deep
Like an ocean floor, forever unfolding and full
I don't believe it
Something so pure and good has never happened to me
Love has never met me and decided to stay
And yet, here you are, holding me as my doubts melt away
Holding me, and continuously, I hear you say,
I love you and I will love you every day
I'm afraid
Scared that one day you'll change your mind

After I've already gone against my better judgment and
given you all of me
After I've already seen my whole life in your arms
After I've already surrendered my entire heart
I've done that before, I've given my heart
And if history repeats itself
Then you'll change your mind at some point, too
You put my palm in yours
Kissed me at the knuckles and looked up to meet my eyes
I began to cry
You met my fear with a loving and understanding smile
You said:

I know you're scared, and through all of that skepticism
and fear that life gave you as a reaction
I will still be here
Loving you throughout each day

Again, you kissed my tears away.

Have you ever loved someone the way that you love me?
Because you love me so perfectly
That it feels like you've had a lifetime of practice
Yet, you give me such a sense of security that I never fear you'd leave me
So, who is she?
Who are the people that make up the path that led you to me?
Cause I wanna say thank you for crafting the man of my dreams
I'm thanking the stars for bringing you to me
My heart is at so much peace when you close your eyes as I rest my hand on your cheek
You are the moment, standing at the edge of the earth, admiring the sea
You're my California dream
My heart doesn't hurt as much anytime you're near me
You love me so perfect, seeing me for me
I wanna say thank you for making your way to me
I wanna say I love you
And my love for you is all-consuming
But you love me so perfectly
You never let me lose my sense of me
I wanna say thank you

For your patience, as I love you ever so clumsily
It's just that, I have never loved anyone the way that I love you
I am pouring my heart and soul into everything for you
Trying to give you peace and ease, too
I'm consulting with the stars, so I can love you as clearly as they do
Holding you and kissing you
Crying tears of gratitude
Have you ever loved someone the way that you love me?
Because I have never loved anyone the way that I love you.

I felt peace, solace; you were the retreat my soul had been
searching
The universe put you before me
And I cry tears of happy
I kissed you
And you kissed me
Your intentions tasted like love and trust
And *I love you, too* rolls off my tongue.

Dreams dance along the entrance of sleep
Waiting patiently to meet me and greet
But never knowing fully that they'll never get to see me
My mind races back and forth until the morning swiftly comes upon me
Until the rising sun begins to warm my bones and create movement in my stiff toes
What I wouldn't give to wake up to a kiss
Rather than toss another turn from my insomnia that never gives
Imagine sleeping soundly curled upon your bed
Fingers intertwined with a warm pair of hands that never let you go all through the night
My leg rests on top of yours and my torso may as well be ours
The way you didn't let me go once in the night
You wrapped your arm around me and held me strong and tight
It wasn't just me; I know you felt it too
I know you felt the safeness in that bed
But you were sleeping too
I know sleep eludes you, misses you by a hair
It waits for you at your bedroom door
But never quite meets you there

Midnight strikes the clock, and we are still sleeping soundly
Only wake to kiss your lips and pull me tighter toward your hips
Maybe this is the dream that waited so patiently for me
Where love making in the cold night warms each other's bones and puts us back to sleep
A safe space in this bed that I have made
Covers to cover our dreams
Kiss me gently and set the scene
Whispering to come closer, as if we aren't already touching
As close as I can get, I reach my hand across the bed
Draped over your chest and fingers tracing along your neck
I really want to kiss your shoulder
A token of gratitude for making me feel this way
Without even trying, this dreamland shifts to reality
Or maybe it's all one and the same, with you I feel cloud nine feelings and grounded feet planted by the seas
All day long you keep me high above the sky
Soaring through clouds and feeling sun on my skin
And in the evenings take me below sea level
Making me wet and keeping me hot despite the winter winds.

In a world where nothing makes sense
And love is a mere facade
I find myself falling deeper into it each day
Call me Alice
Jumping into colorful and wondrous graves
Here in your Wonderland is where I want to stay
Sipping tea, lazily
Knowing damn well, we'll all be late
Throw clocks out the window
As to dance in a timeless rain
When you look about my beautiful
In a sunken eyes kind of way
Sitting on pedestals
And making me feel tall in all the right ways
I could never want to leave
Pull me deeper in your colorful gaze
In this nonsensical world
I enjoy getting lost
Like an Earl Grey latte
Topped with a bit of froth
Smokey plumes fill the air
Call me Alice
Because I think I'd like to stay here.

I will dream of you
Even at 6 am
When my coffee is piping hot
When my lids are slightly weighted
And my mind is not yet racing
I'll dream of you all through the day
In small moments when I'm supposed to be focused
In wild thoughts, I may get lost in space
Small moments in time
Little bits of happiness to break the harsh day
And when the dream ends
I may have to brace
For impact
Because the impact you had
Was impactful and grand
So, I will dream of you
Any given chance
And when nighttime falls
I'll get to dream of you again.

Kiss me with so much conviction on the edge of your lips
That I hang on your words
And I wait for your next steps
Press your lips against my thighs
Slowly, I close my eyes
Slowly, your lips press different points of my body
You make a constellation out of me
I'm dripping with anticipation
Your lips bring about impatience from me
Slowly, my breathing will increase
Slowly, your hand reaches up to hold me
Slowly, my back arches and you fold into me
Slowly, you merge into me
If I was a constellation
Then what are we
Moaning into the sky
Our voices carry
Beautifully painting Aurora Borealis on the night.

Nothing in my life has been without effort
And I think that's why I'm so goddamned happy
Because you came into my life and gave me a taste of what effortless is
You came into my life and I don't find myself struggling to exist
I'm more of myself than I feel like I have ever been
There's an appreciation that I felt settle into my knuckles
Where a tight tension used to feel like a bruise
I feel the pain of having to be relentlessly strong lessen every time I get to hold you
I feel that exhaling is easier
And I don't get the sharp pain in my ribcage
Nightmares are more of a blue moon occasion
And I can fall into sleep quicker than before
My body is experiencing bliss
An effortless I'd never known before this.

"Sometimes, you can be really fuckin annoying, you know that?" We laughed as I spooned peanut butter out of the jar and licked it like it was a lollipop. I was giving him shit for craving pancakes at 2 o'clock in the morning and being upset that we didn't have any whipped cream to top it with.

"You're telling me that you've never had pancakes for dinner? It's the best time to have pancakes." Only it wasn't dinner time anymore, it was a soon-to-be Thursday morning, which made the moment that much more laughable.

When we should be sleeping, we were wide-awake in this small kitchen. The counter was covered with pancake mix, the sink was beginning to overflow with dishes, and Noah was standing at the stove top, handsome as ever.

He was a great cook, a messy cook, but a great one, so I don't doubt that the food will taste good in this limbo hour between night and day.

"What do you mean?" I teased him with a grin, "Of course I have, but that's not what's so funny here. I think it's cute! You want whipped cream on your pancakes, like a little kid." I laugh through the thick peanut butter along my teeth.

"If you want, I can make it into a smiley face too." My smile was wide and taunting as I giggled. I knew I'd never been happier in my life than I was in this moment. There was something about him that made even the most mundane things turn into a moment to live for.

That's what every day felt like with him. But here and now, the world was still and quiet. There was no hum of cars as they passed down the street. The stray cats had long since been to sleep. All I could hear was his scruffy, tired voice—like music—the spoon hitting the sides of the peanut butter jar and us laughing as we clutched our bellies.

After pouring a ladle-full of batter into the pan, he comes over to me as I was sitting on the kitchen counter. Wearing nothing but underwear and his t-shirt, he always made me feel like this is when I was the most beautiful.

As I teased him, he threatened to put peanut butter on my face, grabbing at my hand. I dropped the spoon right onto the floor, "oh, you're gonna clean that." I smiled and teased even more, pointing toward the floor.

With his other hand, he tickled my ribs, and we laughed and laughed until I folded into him, falling into his lips. I loved kissing him, the world stops, as if it was allowing for one moment of absolute perfection in a world of chaos.

His tickling fingers relaxed into a soft caress of my torso. One hand moving from my ribs to the small of my back, while the other held my cheek, finding its way into the tangles of my hair.

I'm not sure what heaven is like, but if I can stay in this moment forever, then I would be more than happy. I would say that I could die after this, that this moment of all moments would leave me satisfied enough that I could die, and my life would have served its purpose—that is, to be entirely consumed by a love that only Noah and I could make. But then, I would miss him too much.

I pulled him closer to me, by wrapping my legs around his torso and my arms over his shoulders; we were warm together. This was what home felt like. We kissed each other's laugh and laughed into each other's kiss.

We made pancakes with no whipped cream, so instead we drizzled chocolate and make a wild fucking mess. It was delicious, the pancakes were decent too.

I imagined that love would change me
That it would strip me of the strength I plastered into my walls
And that all of my boundaries would wash away
I imagined that giving love a chance would end with me in ball of pain, no better than I was years ago
A place and a time I vowed to never revisit
But that wasn't the case at all
My determination, which evolved to stubborn, which led me to resistant
And it wasn't until I gave him a chance that I realized that love didn't have to change me
Love wasn't forceful in nature
It wasn't manipulative in its existence
I was wrong to assume that pure love would mirror anything I had ever seen before
Because this love made me stronger
This love made me hope more, live fearlessly, and love unconditionally
This love gave me a new lens and I would forever cherish the perspective that I get to have now
This love gave me a voice where it was once silenced and misunderstood

This love gave me a clarity that felt like finally breathing in crisp air after a sandstorm
With this love quilted over me, I could feel everything he was and all that I worked toward, stitched together by the memories we created with one another
I imagined love would change me
But never thought it would change me for the better
I imagined love would change me
It did, and now I get to feel this forever.

I want more of him
I know to be selfish is just shy of a sin
But can I sin just a little bit
It surprises me
As I am filled with lust, but more so with greed
I am craving
I am a hot-blooded fiend
I just want more of him
More time
More laughs
More sensual play
More everything
And I want it everyday
I also want less
Less space between us
Less land and less sea
Less pollution blocking the view from him to me
Less time differences
Less texts, less calls
I want less of so many things
But most importantly
And most urgently
I want it all.

Kiss me on the shoulder when you wake in the morning
Wrap your arm around me and pull me in
There's a draft coming in from the window
So, hold on to me
Put your lips on my skin
I'm waking and it still feels like I'm in a dream
Hold on to me
Don't let me go
Don't set me free
This bed is an island
And we're here to enjoy the island breeze
There's a stillness in the air
Where I don't feel the need to rush out the door
And 5am alarms don't bother me anymore
Because every waking second in your arms
Is a second, I've been praying for
Hold on to me
Don't let me go
Don't set me free.

Has there ever been an ocean that never wavered, never pushed, nor pulled? Something with such a magnitude, and yet, beautifully still. Or was this only found in dreams, perhaps in moments quiet when no one in all the world is awake.

Not even mice scurry through the streets, and the birds don't trust fall into the arms of a breeze. Has such a moment ever existed? An anomaly of sorts. That's what it felt like with Noah. Like a wave less ocean, still and quiet, as if the world respected our peace and wanted to bear witness to our love story as it was being written.

Sometimes, I was like that too; sometimes, I was so amazed at the feelings that were holding me that I wanted to take a step back just to watch and see that it was real. But then I'd miss it, and that felt like a crime.

And so, I made a habit to breathe in every moment with him. From the moment my heart knew it was love, my mind instinctively knew to capture each memory and hold it tight forever. Each sunrise and daybreak, each cup of coffee made, and every sip that I can't recall the taste of because it was immediately followed by his lips.

That taste I remember. The coffee was hot and creamy, but he was warm and loving. The coffee was either vanilla or hazelnut, but he was consistent and safety. The taste of his lips felt like a home I'd never stray too far from, while the coffee was replaceable.

So, maybe there is such a thing as wave less oceans, because the way that Noah's heart held mine was a phenomenon that may only happen once in a lifetime. It made me believe that miracles do exist, or that oceans can be still and at peace.

I don't think either one of us strove for perfection. I could tell in the way that we disagreed on small things and big. I didn't think it was bad though because it meant we were staying true to ourselves.

Noah came into this relationship with his beliefs, his morals, and his flaws just as I did. The way that one of us ate on the couch, and the other would never. One of us budgeted more than the other and sometimes, the bathroom got messier than I can stand.

Sharing a space with someone in an intimate way, not a sexual way, but an up-close-and-personal way meant learning a lot about them and even more about yourself. Before, I never had to share space or be considerate of someone else.

I never had to be mindful of what the other person needed or required to breathe easily. I never thought anything of my eating late-night bowls of cereal on the couch as I watched re-runs of episodes that I had seen a dozen times prior.

He never had someone request that he place everything back where he found it in the bathroom. Blending spaces can bring out the worst in people. So, the more time that Noah and I spent together, the more that we learned about each other and ourselves.

The bigger disagreements took more time to work through. Like, not only do I expect help maintaining the home that we had been indulging in as of late, but even more importantly, what were his expectations of my role in this space versus his own roles?

Disagreements over small issues often led to critical thinking sessions over bigger things; things that would inevitably come up had our relationship grew stronger. In order to combat the natural defenses, we would both need a healthy dose of being open-minded.

There would be no other way to continue the way we had been if neither one of us was willing to adapt to each other. We could talk to, and at, each other all day and go nowhere if neither one of us was willing to receive that information.

I would never call what he had arguments. Maybe that was because they never reached volumes like my past had proven possible, or maybe it was because it was an even exchange of dialect.

We both had a voice that was evenly distributed among those discussions. There was compromise and effort at the end, and I will say this. We never had the same discussion about a disagreement twice. And every time that a new disagreement came about, we faced it with patience and respect, just as we had the first one.

It was the precise act of care that showed me no matter what we didn't see eye to eye on, we could get to common ground eventually.

I think this is the part of love that I was never so lucky to experience before. Where my voice was not only heard but appreciated. Where, I not only was encouraged to speak my truth, but he also took every word to heart, and we found resolution together.

I knew I'd always give him the same respect. He had earned that, and he deserved an open and honest partner that could communicate this stuff to him. As hard as it was for me to get the words out, I tried my best.

Past experiences always shut me down, so I never felt it safe or even my right to make my opinion known. But now, our opinions danced together, and we learned, and we grew. So far, we'd established common ground and compromised on every fine line we'd crossed.

Sometimes, I gave a little, and sometimes, he gave a little. It was a constant ebb and flow of forgiveness, grace, and understanding. There was no greed in the decisions made, nor was there selfish intentions.

There was longevity and promise. There was understanding in that, these decisions were the foundation for something greater, so they needed to be strong and indeed they were.

I think people have idolized true love so long that when the
potential of love sits before you, you haven't a clue that it's
there
I think love is rocky at first
It quivers on its tip toes
Shakes at the feeling when a rough wind blows
It may fall to its roots
But truth is in the waiting as the tree still continues to grow
We forget that love takes time
The deepest love isn't formed through a first look through
the eyes
It's a gaze that lasts long enough for your eyes to water
The need to blink and refresh your lens
And then
Choose to continue gazing at your partner
Love is quivering lips at first
Delicate in the sense that we mustn't rush
And perfection is learned
In asking for permission to taste another's world
The sentiment that drips from one's lips
Becomes the taste the other craves
And love blooms like flowers from the mouth
On beautifully sunny spring days
Love is slowly coming out of a drought

Wandering deserts for months
And realizing your skin is supple now
You're not parched nor dehydrated
At some point, it must have rained
The sky cried for you
Now desert flowers can bloom again
Love is imperfect
Emotions as fluid as the seas
Uncertain and unearthing
But you still wish to meet it at the shore
And watch as the sea salt washes over your feet
Love is love is love is love
And when you have it, and when you're knee-deep
Recall the journey
And how it's nothing like what they teach.

If she and I were characters on a keyboard, there would instinctively be an ampersand between our names, because we were meant to be together. For the rest of my life, I can never be *just* Noah again.

If there's no her, then I'm certain there's no me. In what felt like a short time, I felt like I had lived my life to its fullest with her. I'd seen the world through the most beautiful lens and learned a heart that I didn't feel worthy of.

She doesn't know it yet, but I'm going to marry her. I'm going to fall in love with her and if I'm lucky enough, I'll get to see her on her worst days, just as much as her best days.

She told me once that she doesn't ever feel good enough, and she doesn't feel like she deserves good things. I don't understand how such a beautiful mind and selfless soul could ever be undeserving, but I'm going to spend my days refilling her.

It was being with her that made me realize that I'd never actually been in love before. And there wasn't just one reason why I thought I loved her. She was the most beautiful woman I'd ever seen, but that's not why.

She made me want better for myself. I saw her wake up every day and prioritize her need for self-care and love, I saw her love herself through education and art, I saw her take care of herself and still find it in herself to want to care for me too.

After filling her own cup, she wrapped her arms around me, on the tips of her toes, and filled me up too. She was compassionate and whole, even though she recalled all of her broken days.

She was kindness and enthusiasm in a world where everyone selfishly cheered for themselves. Her heart was so pure, she made me want to be a better man and be one that deserved a heart like that.

***

Noah was something you never saw coming. Because who got that lucky—to meet someone like him, in a world like this, in a city like ours, on a day like that? And of all the faces that day, all the people, he bumped into me, and he saw me, and wanted to take me out for coffee.

I was really not sure how it happened, but I'm happy it did. I'm almost not even scared of what could become of this. If anything, only scared that one day, it will have ended. I would be okay if it did, but I can't say with confidence that my heart would survive it.

But that's not the case, because I got really lucky to meet someone like him, in this world, in my city, on that day. The moment we locked eyes I knew something beautiful was going to happen. I had ignored my gut before, but I listened this time, and she was singing the most beautiful song I'd ever heard.

I knew that he and I were meant for something more, like the stars had been conspiring for us to meet that day. On the nights that I can't sleep, I lie there, imagining a world where he and I grow together, getting older and living in our age, smiling in our laugh lines, and loving in our experiences.

I imagine a world where we came together at the end of the day and every single night—sleepless or not, dreamless or vivid—we were with each other. I'd be lying if I said I didn't imagine a future with him because I do. *And it's perfect.*

So, I met this woman, right?
Who's got this son
Whose smile shines like moonlight
Who's got his mother's soul
And his grandfather's calloused hands, right?
Something about his charm
Threw me off guard
Cause I kinda think I'd like to end up in a spot where we could talk
And a light would ignite
Cause maybe a few years down the line
I find myself at his side
Or maybe at the bedside
I find a little mini him
Who runs up to me, looking at me with his eyes
Wearin' the same soul from his paternal grandmother's side
Maybe we find ourselves dancing in the kitchen past midnight
Waking to mornings that hold promise and insight
And when we visit his mother
She looks at me and smiles
Says she loves to have me as a daughter
I thank her for loving me
And as family we embrace in laughter

Maybe a couple years longer
There's a daughter of our own
Who wears my eyes
And he holds her like she's fit to hold a throne
And in these moments
Where my son with the soul
Smiles into the sunset and says he thinks it's beautiful
And my husband holds our daughter
And vows to never let her go
I find myself smiling
Thinking back to the day
That I met this woman, right?
Turns out she had this son
Whose smile shines like moonlight.

I wasn't done yet

I wasn't done feeling him warm me at the ribcage

Like I was at a campsite, cold under the stars

And he was a burning flame

Eyes as entrancing as wild embers, and a touch just the same

I wasn't done stealing his hot and bothered kisses

Ravenously biting them from his delicious lips

I wasn't done pressing my tongue on his

I wasn't done moaning into this void where nothing mattered, and nothing made sense

All I needed was

The taste of his kiss on the exhale of my breath

The press of his lips on the bare of my chest

The lust of our bodies slowly increase

The hold on my hips as he pulls to me

The bite of his shoulder when my legs straddle each side

The motion swaying like an ocean tide

The shores get wetter and he's going for a deep-sea dive

The press of his lips on my inner thigh

The moaning and screaming long through the night

His hands from the small of back running up and down my sides

Fingertips overcome with greed, gripping me tight

As if they weren't done yet either, gently looking for a longing fight.

My heart and mind have spoken time and time again
Ensuring concurrence
On this touchy subject
I ask if we're in love
And my heart says *yes*
I ask if he's the one
To which my brain says *of course* with an obvious bliss
My gut calmly nods along
So, why is it sometimes, there's this voice in my head that
can't possibly be mine
Who whispers in the background saying he doesn't love me
I fight the thought because I know it isn't true
But the voice is getting louder
And I might start to believe her too
You ever get that?
When your defenses get defensive over nothing at all
When you're safely in your haven
And your fight or flight kicks on
But you don't have any fight left in you
So, you think a little too quickly and impulsively
Next thing you know, you're out the door
Throwing everything away
Because it's easier than mending another heartache
Only the overthinking is overcompensating

And there isn't anything to run from
It's just a wave of anxiety that sounds like past mistakes
And this safe haven that's so warm and so new
Is something that feels untrusting because you never knew
how to exist in something like this?
Living in chaos only gives question to the calm
So, you start packing
Because you begin to confuse safety for the storm
You convince yourself that the love blocks you're standing
on
Are shaking in its façade
That everything you'd built is a mere mirage
You believe history and false tales in your mind
And then forget to breathe and bring yourself back to the
present time.

***

I got home from work and found that everything was quiet; all the lights were off. Usually, she's home by now and almost always had the record player on. Her favorite was this Prince record, no idea why, there's only about 4 songs on it. But she heard magic in it.

But today everything is off and she was in the back, and there's no music, only a cry. A loud sobbing sound, so I rushed to get to her.

"What's wrong? Where are you going? What are you doing?"

She's throwing shit into bags so fast that I don't even think she realized that she only had shirts in that bag. The more I look at her, the more I see how hurt she is. Her eyes look bloodshot, red and swollen. She's hyperventilating and crying, wiping her face and angry.

She has keys in her hand and she's frantic with a bit of desperation. Desperately trying to leave. I can't quite paint it, but she looks terrified, like she's in survival mode. Like someone held her voodoo doll and whispered in her pierced ears, *run*.

"Baby, talk to me, what happened today, why are you leaving?"

She can't get the words out, just crying, rushing, crying, and packing.

"Cause, I'm fucked up," she finally screams. "I saw him today, or at least I think I did. And everything he ever said, everything he ever did came flooding back into my mind. He may as well be dead, but he's fucking everywhere I look, and what if everything he said was wrong, but what if it's not?"

"You don't deserve someone like that, like this, like me! You deserve someone soft and fresh and unbroken. You deserve someone who gives you a clean slate, not someone whose half convinced she's a shit person. I'm sorry, I gotta go, I just need to—"

She looked defeated. Absolutely fucking wrecked, whatever happened in her past life—the one she lived before me—haunts her. And today, it was too much for her. Uncontrollably sobbing on the floor, her face is buried in her hands.

"I'm sorry, I want to love you so much, and I want you to love me too, but I'm sorry, I gotta go. I can't be here."

So, I met her on the floor, I put my arms around her and now, she's slumped over my lap. She's crying, but I can feel her breathing level out through my denim jeans.

"I'm sorry, I'm sorry I'm so fucked up," Hazel continued to apologize through her tears.

"You're not baby, you just needed a minute. Let's sit here for a minute. I'm here. I'm here with you, and I'm not going anywhere. Whatever he said to you, it isn't true. You are my clean slate, you are meant for me, and you know how I know that?"

"Because it's nothing in this world that makes me happy the way that your smile does. It's nothing that feels better than waking up next to you. It's nothing I want more than I want you. I want tomorrow with you, and a week from now with you."

"I want next year with you, and five years from now with you. You don't get it, Hazel. I got one plan for the rest of my life and it's to make sure that you're beside me. Just talk to me baby, don't run."

"Every fear you have, every tear you cry, talk to me; when your face is puffy and red like that, when you're convinced that you'll run away without me and only wear shirts because you didn't pack any pants."

She looked around, noticing that she really didn't grab any pants and chuckled through her scattered breathing. "When you feel like this again, you just gotta talk to me, I'll calm those fears and I'll remind you that, that voice in your head is a fucking liar. Cause I do love you, Hazel. I'm gonna love every bit of you, and there isn't one damn thing you can show me that would change that," I said definitively.

"Besides, if you're running, I'm running too. I'm in this with you."

So, we sat there, in a mess of shirts, on the floor. My hands surfed through the waves of her hair. Her eyelids grew heavy, and she eventually dropped the keys from her hands, nail polish chipping on her fingertips.

And we sat there. She opened up her wounds and told me what she feared most, and things she wrongfully believed. I kissed her wounds and told her otherwise. She took a deep breath, and that day, learned that she never had to feel like she had to run away again. Not while I was around.

***

Learning you, will always mean learning me too
It'll be building a trust between us both
A bond that can be so easily lost
That's why when all this feels so good
I shake in my shoes and question the intentions and occurrences between us too
I find myself questioning my judgment,
because I loved before and it ended abruptly
But I look you in the eyes and it feels right each and every time
The trust I had for my own gut was broken a time or two
And then on top of that, I have to learn to trust you too
It can be a little overwhelming when I really think about it
A lot to process, and you can see that whole process written on my face
Cause my canvas is so transparent

I couldn't hide a feeling or emotion throughout a single day
To settle those complexities inside
I find myself focusing on what's real and what's right
What's true and what's mine
What happened last night
Exact moments when you supported my need for you
Met me in the shadows and started a fire, so I can see the
light too
Patient when I was stubborn and graceful when I'm clumsy
When I focus on what happened and what's real
The words you say and how the actions are mirrored
Then I find that trust being rebuilt
Between your heart and mine.

Living

Maybe love is gracious enough to taste the apology left over
in my depression
The good morning kiss says, I know you were up all night
That in your dreams, you couldn't stop crying
But now that you're awake, just know I'm here and you're
alright
Maybe love is patient enough to look me in the eyes and
level my breathing as I only inhale shakily inside
Tells me to exhale slowly and close my eyes
Take as long as you need
I'm right by your side
Maybe love sounds like a collection of the youthful days I
thought I lost long ago
Laughter bouncing off the walls
Smiles turn to echoes
Wrinkle lines set into the creases of our eyes
And we wipe away happy tears cried
Maybe love is stealing things off your plate
When I don't think you're looking
I take the stress from your day
Only to find, you've taken my pain and aches
Balancing each other, so we can restart when we wake

Maybe love is sleeping soundly for once
Or feeling calmness in the sound of your voice
Or feeling motivated by watching you work
Or getting messy, as we build a life from the dirt
Maybe love is simple and easy
Where we are a team
Both wanting to create reality from our dreams
Where you feel supported and held
And your mind body and soul can safely exhale
Where there are no walls built for fear and protection
Where we are long past the days of skepticism and rejection
Maybe love is comfort and eyes closed
Swinging on a hammock
Wind breezes on our toes
Maybe love is possible
That a reality like this is plausible
And a man like you I could call home
That you would be reliable, excitable, tangible.

He was a tall, brooding man. The crease in his brow tells me that he had war stories that he never dared to speak about. But I can feel, when he's relaxed, that he is softer. And it showed when his smile grew wide. All mystery floated out the window, carried on a breeze that carried the scent of his cologne.

He was a beautiful man, not because of his dark thick eyelashes that framed his eyes. Not because of his posture, the way he carried such a heavy world with poise and grace on his big, broad shoulders. And not because of the way he always managed to look at me—not through me, not with intentions—but just to see me.

He was wonderful in the sense that, despite all that he's ever been through, he is still kind. I want to say that I fell in love with him when I saw the way he interacted with the little old man on the park bench.

Or maybe I loved him the day that I saw how delicate he was with children, wildly imaginative and carefree. Quite possibly, I fell in love with him when I saw his protective side. He roared at the world, and I never felt safer.

It wasn't in a scary way, and not in a way that alerted me to run. He felt like what I imagined safety felt like in that moment, and I wanted to stick by his side ever since. It was hard to pinpoint the moment that I fell, because it was how the days went by with him, it was a cascading descent in the most artistic sense, where love was waiting for me at every breaking point.

Like the day he was delicate with me. The day he carried my face in his big palms and sat on the floor without hesitation. I was lost and melting in a sea of my own dark seas, and he was the lifeboat. He came for me, and he carried me back to safety without ever making me feel ashamed for drowning in the first place.

He had that way about him. With his few friends, his younger siblings, his mother, he was a shoulder to everyone. And never once asked for anything in return. And that just made me love him even more. Honestly, it made me want to be his shoulder too.

This tall, brooding man, with a heart of gold—what happened to you? What happened along the way that you're so mysterious? He'd never say it was an issue, he'd never admit to needing help, the way that I wear that need for help on my sleeve. He was the strong one, effortlessly so.

He was also extremely kind and smart. As I wrote in the evenings, he read. He will lie on the left side of the bed, a book held up in his right hand and his left hand raised behind his head, comfortably lying beside me.

I started by sitting up on the opposite side of the bed, but as I exhausted the thoughts, I set down my pencil, I lay on his chest, and I exhaled until I fell asleep. He will always finish his chapter, and that was bliss. A moment to live for, I guess any moment with him would be a moment to live for.

His eyes were a home away from home, we don't even have to say a word, but I could live there for the rest of my life. They were colored, a mix of olive and emerald, a world of its own. And when he smiled, there were creases at the corners of them.

He lit up, so you'd never know that he was as serious as he is. He often had calloused hands, even though he had a delicate touch, he'd been working every day of his life since he was 15 years old.

I'd loved nothing more than getting to know him inside and out. He was a genuinely good person and I felt like I stumbled upon him. I was past the point of resistance and questioning.

Past the point of wondering how and why, or if it was true or not, and I was where I just wanted to be with him, exist with him, live fully with him, and make memories with him. This is where we grow together, and wherever the adventure takes us, I'm a willing passenger.

It's not every day that I get to be so lucky
That I get to know a truth so raw and a love so pure
Hold a hand so tight that my world shifted from a dull,
mundane to a bright beautiful light
And all I have to do is make up my mind
Each morning light
Commit to loving your flaws the way that you protect mine
Accept your heart, the way you've always accepted mine
Understand your soul, and appreciate the complexities of
your mind
And I do
I would choose you every day of this lifetime
Every step I ever will take, predestined to meet you at the
finish line
Loving you like art, protecting your smile
And in five years' time
When you've shed your perspective and look at the world
through new eyes
Or fifty years, or when I'm old and blind
I'd love you same, if not more, than this moment in time
If I could right now, I'd make you my wife
Cause every single day, I'd choose you
Every day till we close eyes and then even more, a thousand
times

I'd love this version of you, and the reinvented versions that will come later down the line.

I love your steady and your calm
Your hands float to me
Sweeping the hair from across my chin
It was a merciful movement
Whatever it was, you always understood it
One that I melt in
If you were ever nervous when your eyes met mine
I never noticed
Falling between the spaces of words never spoken
Replaced by kisses and moaning
I fell for you
For the man you said you were
Steady and calm.

When we hold hands
And our forearms kiss
It's like I plant sunflowers in your skin
And suddenly, you're a garden
In human form
I think I found something like love in you
And I could mostly tell
Because your eyes are the color of a broken trauma cycle
And your lips whisper affirmations that I must've loved
myself more this time
Because I attracted a path that led me to you
Who was love in human form.

I forgot what my love language was because you satisfied me in all five tongues. But my favorite was when you looked me in the eyes, and I got to embrace your *touch*. And I'm not sure that I was ever a physical touch kind of lover, but the safety and warmth that you put on my body has me craving your love every morning.

I thought I was an *acts of service* kind of person, and it reminded me how you took care of me when I was hurting. How you offered your help when I was struggling. And it's in those moments of completeness that I am certain.

Until you sit across the table from me in the mornings and we laugh over breakfast, this time is of the purest *quality*. Now I know why they say breakfast is the most important meal of the day.

But then I get lost in the things you *say*, reassuring my distance from my fears that there's nothing to worry about here. Painting my face with the syllables you speak, beautiful and yours.

That's when I decided that you're a *gift*. Somehow filling every cup that I didn't know I had.

What love language is that?

I often wondered if I was loving Noah the way he deserved. He was effortlessly showing me affection, safety, and beauty all at once, and I so clumsily resisted it as I convinced myself that I was allowed to be loved the way he was consistently doing so.

I held onto so much of what'd been left behind me, that I forgot to let it go, and sometimes that got in the way of this newness that I was in with him. Sometimes, it prevented me from seeing everything for what it was. And it is sweet, it is so kind to me, it is surely more than anything I could have ever deserved.

Noah saw something in me that I spent years convincing myself wasn't there. He saw a home, and I was a gypsy. I never knew stable the way he insisted it, yet he was here, stable and steady.

I found myself at a point where I wanted to tell him that I was *all in*. I wanted to be able to look him in the eyes and let him know that my shortcomings were mine alone, and I would never ask him to take ownership, but I also can't promise that he will never have to experience them.

I wanted to tell him that one hundred percent of my heart was covered in tattoos of his name, in all different fonts because I was committed to making it look as beautiful as he was.

But with the same tongue, I needed to also say that there wasn't much left of a heart like mine at the end of the day. Even though I knew that he would respond with something along the lines of, "shut up," with a chuckle, "that's crap. Your heart, and every piece you think is broken, is the most beautiful heart I've ever seen. You don't have to know that yet, but I know it, and I'll know it enough for the both of us."

I wanted to let him know that I was scared, I had fears so deeply in my bones that I didn't remember life before them. It was not that I wanted him to share in my fears or coddle them, I didn't even want him to live with them, just to know that sometimes, we may have uninvited guests— trauma living in the attic of our one-day home.

Most urgently, I wanted him to know that I loved him. I was so deep in a world that I had never known, so it must be love. And I loved it more than anything because I was here with him. To which he would kiss me. He wasn't a man of many words, but the ones he plucked from the sky were always so perfect and so fitting for any moment.

Before, when I found myself second-guessing, it would manifest into knots in my stomach, and I would have this ball of anxiety sitting in the pit of it all. But now, I didn't second guess what was happening. I see him and I know. I see us and I know. I feel us, and I know.

***

It's as if I could sleep for all my years
I was always restless and needed to close my eyes

164

The days went past me, and I was running just to maintain momentum
All the while, just wanting to stop
Just wanting to catch my breath under the willow trees
Leaning on the earthy bark, as I catch the smell of flowers on a tide-like breeze
I craved stillness in perpetuity
Where my strength wasn't a prerequisite for each morning light
Where success wasn't determined by wins and losses by fight
Where movement was as fluid as a dancing fire
But it always seemed to move right past me
I never got to feel that serenity
Because I was always surrendering to an endless cycle
I was always so strong, having done so much
Having met so many demons and fought so many wars
Having picked myself back up
From being exhausted on all fours
Having been so restless, yet overcoming adversity
I just knew after all this I craved stillness
I craved calm and safe, in perpetuity
Then I met you
And I notice my sleep is deeper than before
I'm living through my dreams now
Not just waiting for them along the door
I can slow down enough to catch my breath without fear
I can move toward dreams and goals with the sound of your motivation in my ear
I can stop as I please, and I can feel safe enough to sleep, all because you're here

I'm living in the safety I craved, I'm basking in the sunrays
as they touch me
I'm living and loving in perpetuity.

It was late in the afternoon and I was home from work, Hazel was supposed to be here soon and would let herself in with the key that was hidden under the doormat. So, I took that time to shower and straighten up my very lived in apartment.

Afterwards, I started to cook something for us to eat, when I heard the key in the door. Hazel walked in with a big purse on one arm, a lunchbox and an oversized water bottle in the other, and somehow, she also had her phone in her hand.

I saw her walk in as this chaotic hurricane, beautiful in the way that only nature could be. She walked in as if she had been there a million times before and this was part of her daily routine, because in one fell-swoop, she kicked off her shoes at the door and dropped all of her bags on the first chair she saw.

With a big smile on her face, she came up to me and put both arms around my shoulders, "hi baby," and planted a kiss on my lips. She then started walking toward the bedroom and before she made it past the door, her raised arms were removing her shirt.

Before I knew it, her bra was on my bed. "I am so hungry," she said from inside the room, loud enough for me to hear the emphasis on the *so hungry* by extending her syllables. I can hear her shuffling around, in and out of tunes.

Though I couldn't make out the songs she was singing, I could hear that she'd had a good day. She emerged from my room wearing my t-shirt. Her hair had been in a bun all day, but now, thick curls hung past her shoulders.

The smell of chicken teriyaki and steamed vegetables filled the air, and Hazel, as full of life as she is, was dancing around the kitchen to the music she continued to hum. As she went about the details of her day, I listened intently and felt her energy absorbing into my soul.

She was really comfortable around me, in my home, and in my life. I saw her reach on the tips of her toes for the black pepper to add to the vegetables as she asked me how my day was. During what feels like a dance party in the kitchen, we talked about the ins and outs of the hours we were apart.

She managed to accomplish a lot at work today, while I managed to finish one of my biggest projects to date. She spilled an entire cup of coffee this morning, so that's why her shoes look that way. *Not that I looked down to even notice the stain on them.*

I had a few energy drinks today, so that was why I was drinking tall glasses of water now. She hung on to me as the food finished up its last several minutes of cooking time. Her hair smelled sweet, as always, and I could feel her smile pressed into my chest.

I could get used to this, coming home to each other and talking about our day. I could see her coming down from her adrenaline rush and dancing to music that only she could hear.

She steals my shirts off the hangers as if they were hers. This wasn't a life that is ours yet, but if we try hard enough, then maybe, one day it will be.

Tonight, I had a surprise for Hazel. I got tickets to some big fancy art gallery opening. Hopefully, this will excite her, because I don't know anything about famous artists. I can barely tell the difference between watercolor and oil paints, but Hazel was smarter than me, she loved to read and loved music more than anything else. So, maybe, art was pretty high up there for her too.

"Wow! That's so exciting!" she exclaimed when I handed her the tickets. "Some friends of mine would have loved this, I can't believe you got tickets." As she read on, she mentioned the dress code, the time it started and the location.

"Oh, my goodness, this is so fancy, I hope I have something that will work for this. I think the fanciest place I go to is that pasta place that we both like," she laughed in nervous excitement.

As we both got ready for our date tonight, I wore a black suit with my hair being persuaded in all the right directions by the last of my pomade. I spritzed just enough of my cologne, Hazel's favorite scent, on me.

There wasn't much for me to do to get ready because I didn't think there was anything special that I owned or could use to get all fancy. But Hazel, on the other hand, stepped out wearing a satin dress the color of deep green emeralds.

I'd never seen her wear this dress before, but after tonight, I would never forget it. It loosely hugged her curves in all the right places, with a slit up the left leg that showed her thigh. She wore gold heels with a single strap around the ankle and a white shawl around her shoulders.

Her hair was tied up with a few fallen curls to frame her face while these gold earrings dangled near her neck. She was beautiful every single day, but tonight, she was glowing in it, the type of beauty that catches you in your throat when you try to speak to it.

"Do I look okay?" she questioned. The worry lines tried to settle their way around her eyes, so I tried to convince them away.

"You look," I struggled to find the words that would do her justice, "striking, magnificent, like the most beautiful person there was." I could see her blushing under her makeup.

"And you look as handsome as ever." She smiled and kissed my cheek.

When we arrived, there were a lot more people that showed up than I imagined. "I'm kind of nervous," she said.

"Why babe?"

"I don't know, there's just a lot of people here." We walked back and forth between beautifully executed art pieces; paintings, sculptures, and interactive display pieces. She and I were impressed with each and every one.

To no surprise, I hadn't a clue who any of these artists were and Hazel only knew a small handful. It was quite the experience, nonetheless. More people flooded in, and I could feel Hazel's presence beginning to tense. Crowds weren't her thing, and I didn't blame her.

They weren't mine either, but at least this crowd was subdued and calm. The overall ambience was peaceful and tranquil. Amid the movement and the few glasses of wine we'd each had, I swear I heard Hazel's stomach growl.

I looked at her questioningly, and her blush returned under her makeup. It was close to midnight now, and I knew that almost nothing was open at this hour.

"This place is great and all," she whispered to me through a slightly drunk giggle, "but they are passing out bites of food, like, crackers and hummus. Baby, if it can fit on a toothpick, it's not gonna do the job."

I couldn't help but laugh at her declaration. It was time that the art show ended, and we left, because I was getting hungry too.

It was a beautiful night and the wine convinced us to go for a walk and make an adventure out of this date. The tension had left her body and her smile was rich with happiness. We talked about the pieces we saw and even marveled at the interactive pieces.

Her favorites were the ones with the most color, and mine were the complete opposite. I didn't learn a single artist's name all night because even though I was surrounded by paintings all night, I found myself stealing glances at Hazel.

"Baby! A taco truck!" Of course, she would spot a taco truck, the flashing lights reeled her in. "I'll take three chicken tacos and two asada tacos—baby," she looked at me, "do you want anything?"

I was only slightly amazed that she ordered five tacos for herself, but even still knowing her appetite, the shock was still there.

"I guess I'll just have the same," and handed my debit card over, knowing these were going to be some good tacos.

"I need at least—" I cut her off, because I knew exactly what she was about to say. "I know, at least like 7 salsa verde cups for yourself."

She smiled a bashful, yet unapologetic smile. It was always those 2am hours with us when magic happened. Only now, we were sitting on the curb, in our fanciest outfits, eating street tacos. Her gold heels catching a reflection from the taco truck lights.

Even after hours in her makeup and dress, she was still a dream. I slurped the last of the soda, hearing the emptiness at the bottom of the straw. Down to my last taco, I knew tonight was a night to remember. We were both beginning to yawn into our final bites.

The buzz had worn off and our bellies were full. We could have just come straight to this curb and had the same good time, but I'm glad about how the night turned out. The cab that I called had arrived and it was time to head back to her place, I knew she couldn't wait another minute to take off her shoes.

There's magic in the mundane, simply put
I know this sounds unrealistic
That love should speak volumes and feel like fireworks
That love and life should be climactic
Even cinematic
A movie, or a time to be had
That everything we do or invest in another being
Is photo worthy, a reel waiting to be made
But let me tell you about the mundane
Let me tell you about how sweet it feels to know you have
someone to call
Even when you don't have anything to say at all
How beautiful it is to be held in all the right ways
Or to know that you have a place to place your tears when
they fall
Only to be received by sweet intentions and grace
Let me tell you how sweet it is to know your trauma has
been heard
Deep conversations that hang on every star
Your fears and your worries have been placed on the back
of a bird
So that you can exhale and feel safe again
Because you put down the weight of the world
There's beauty in the mundane
Simply put.

I think my favorite part of life right now was the feeling of being whole. Any past roadblocks that I held onto didn't seem to be in the way anymore. I felt full in my sense of self, grounded in a way that I hadn't been in a very long time.

Joyous in a way that felt authentic and pure. I felt free and proud of the life I was living. Maybe it was not because of Hazel, but it was definitely influenced by her. She persuaded a spark in me and now everything lit up.

Her essence and drive, drove me as well. I didn't feel absorbed by her but enhanced with her. It was a wild feeling, scintillating in all its facets. At the end of the day, we came together, and our separate lives melted into one another.

"I just don't get it," Hazel said after taking a full bite of spaghetti while we talked about our day over dinner. "He can't just treat me like I don't know how to do my job. I mean, we have the same position, same duties, same everything, but he seriously just mansplains everything. It's so condescending!"

"Screw that babe, you know exactly what you're doing, he's probably just overcompensating because he knows that if doesn't try to show out in front of you, he'd be out of a job soon." I tried to support her because I knew this wasn't something to be fixed, it was just a needed session of venting.

"He's just so frustrating, he acts like he's hot shit, but really, there are areas he can improve, and I'm sure he knows it."

"Well then, why don't, with all that brain in your head, educate him. Be the boss you are, show out. Do it in front of other people too for a little touch of satisfaction. Everyone knows that you are good at what you do, don't let him shit on that." She knew she was badass, sometimes we all just needed a reminder.

"Ugh, you're right, you're right. He's a dick, I'm fantastic, and that's that!" She said, trying to be as smug as possible, but even her smugness came off as aspiring and confident.

She was too humble to be anything otherwise. I knew she would return to work with just as much grace as the day before, professional and humble.

"But what about your day? Did that annoying customer come back?" She encouraged my need to vent too.

"Sure did, insisting he knew how to fix the damn car. Bossing people around, barking orders. I was so sick of it. I asked him if he knew what to do, then why he brought his car to us. If he knew what to do, then why pay an expert to do it? Gave him his keys and told him to take his car and go. I wasn't about to have him yelling at all of my employees all day long."

"Good for you babe! People like that are so ridiculous, I'm sure he can find someone else to put up with his attitude, and if not, he can try to do it himself, since he's such an expert," Hazel mocked the potential of this guy's ability, and we laughed it off.

Before we knew it, dinner was done and plates were nothing but pasta sauce and breadcrumbs, but we sat there talking for hours anyways. Our frustration toward the day had become our laughter and joke of the night.

A glass of wine became the bottle, and our laughter grew, echoing off the walls of her small apartment. We washed and rinsed the dishes together, our bare feet side by side and soap bubbles getting on the countertops.

Normal things, like dishes and work and cleaning were brought to life with us at each other's side. She was a light that made the mundane less dark, and I was thankful for the view. We could do this; I knew we could.

After we finished up in the kitchen, we both showered off the day and changed into the comfiest of clothes. We put something mindless on the TV because we just weren't done laughing.

My lips found hers and with great relief, her lips were looking for mine too. Those comfy clothes were soon on the floor, but we didn't get cold. The smiles that were once on our lips were bitten with excitement. It felt like love was being made in this room tonight.

Her curls spread over the pillows and fingers stretched outward, she resembled art, and I wanted to feel every piece of the sculpture that she was. My hand was on top of hers, and together, we pressed into the mattress.

I could feel the sweat beginning to wet her hair as I was kissing her along her silhouette. At her earlobe, my teeth gently bit, and my lips moved down to her neck. I could feel her hips moving with mine as her moans were playing in my ear.

In this moment, we embraced each other and pushed and pulled until the moans filled the room. Now, she was on top of me, I can feel her back arch as my hands caressed her body.

She reached for my hand and gripped tightly. Her stride got faster, smoother and faster, faster and smoother. Moans became screams, only broken by heavy breathing and whispers of 'I love you'.

Her body and my body became one; moving together, feeling together, speaking the same language. For a regular Thursday that started out as a headache, it sure didn't end that way.

It was because she was light, and she always seemed to make the mundane less dark. To me, this is what living really was. Every day was intentional, it was fulfilling and grand in its small, regular ways.

We worked well together in so many ways that every time we made magic, it was apparent that we were made for each other. That we were crafted from the same stars, the same sky, and the same setting sun.

Loving

I walked into the room to see what she was up to. The lights were on and the fan was blowing at medium speed; it was the middle of summer and that was a godsend to have.

I found her there, on the not-too-small bed, with a book cracked wide open and her eyes so heavy they must have forced her to sleep.

She was a reader at heart, more books than I could count. And she loved them all, classic literature, spiritual, fiction, horror, mystery. Her mind was as expansive as the ocean. And I loved swimming through it, day in and day out. She was a vast sea, and I was a longtime admirer.

She was beautiful in this moment; peaceful. All the tension melted off her face and surrounded her in her dark pool of hair. I wonder what she was dreaming. *If she was dreaming.*

For a split second, I imagined five years from now. This exact same moment, except our bed grew, her book collection grew, and instead of a book napping by her side, I'd find a little mini-Hazel next to her.

I imagined that maybe, just maybe, I'd done something amazing enough in this life or a past life, that someone, somewhere thought it appropriate to bless me with more of

Hazel. More of her gray-brown eyes. More of her dark, curly hair. More of her smile and laugh. Just more.

I didn't want to get too greedy, and I didn't want to jinx it, but from that moment on, I knew I just wanted more of her. Sleeping soundly and peacefully. I just wanted more. So, I crawled in bed beside her, moved the book to the end table being sure not to lose her page.

I wrapped my arm around her, kissed her nose and whispered into the air that I loved her. I said, "one day, I want a family with you."

I closed my eyes and tried my hardest to find her in whichever dream she was in, because I just wanted more of her.

***

Before I ever met her, I didn't picture what the future might look like, I knew there would be a me, a maybe and that was really it. Maybe I'd have more financial freedom, maybe I'd be with someone, maybe I'd have a kid or two.

But that was it, it was a vague set of maybes that I didn't get too attached to. But when Hazel walked into my life, she flipped the switch and lit up my imagination. Because now I can see it, I can see what I want the future to look like.

I can see the home I picture us in, enough bedrooms for us, the three kids, and a family guest room. I can see the yard that they'll play in—a playset that I'd build myself that had a slide and swings and monkey bars.

I can see the dog running around with the ball. I can see the family dinners, the vacations, the contentment, and bliss on everyone's face. And I loved it.

These were the thoughts that I thought of as I lay next to Hazel. I thought of where life was now, versus where it was a few years ago. Then, I was just existing, and here we were living so deep in love. I wanted to be a provider in a way that I had never had the urge to be before.

I let these thoughts enter and pass through my mind, my patience and impatience battling as I pictured these moments. As I did this, I felt Hazel toss and turn, as she normally did. Usually, she will wake at least once throughout the night.

I knew that Hazel was something special from the moment we met, but right now, I can't help but really think of our growth together. I loved that she knew she could trust me, I'd never let a thing happen to her.

I was so confident in what I felt for her, and confident that she felt the same for me. We became a unit over time, a team, and together, a force. I didn't even know it, but this feeling was what I had wanted for a long time.

I could feel Hazel moving around again, only this time waking slightly. The room was dark and the only other sound besides my inner dialogue, was the fan blowing toward us.

"Honey"
I love when she whispers to me in the dead of night
She complains about being tired
But would always rather stay up late
"Yeah, babe?"
"I love you, can you hold me?"
And in that moment, I know she's longing for something
And even now, it's hard for her to say that
It's hard for her to need me
Because everyone she's ever needed
Left without speaking
So, I wrap my arms around her
Let her know I haven't gone anywhere
I'm here and if we stay up until 3am every morning
Then that's okay with me
She closes her eyes
With her heavy head on my chest
And drifts to sleep
It's not that she needed me there
But she felt safe in my arms
So, in my arms, is where I always wanted her to be
She deserved safe
After all she's been through
And I wanted to spend my whole life

Giving her that feeling
So, I whisper "I love you too baby."
Kiss her forehead
And we sleep.

My dad didn't get my mom a home. He wasn't there at all, so I swore that if I ever fell in love, I'd make sure that my wife would have one. And Hazel; well, she wasn't my wife yet, but she was someone that I would do anything for.

She deserved someone to love her so much that they would get her a home. The kind that was safe and secure and never rumbled when things were shaky inside. She was so good, like a little slice of heaven was cut out of the sky and somehow, I walked into it.

I honestly don't know how I got so lucky, but I thank God every day that I did. I looked up to the stars every night and asked each one how to love her best and if there was a way that I didn't know of to love her better.

She only ever gave to people; she only thought of how to help someone else. And I don't remember the last time she asked for anything in return. So, each time I was blessed enough to wake up beside her, I wanted to make sure that I can give to her because she is good.

Kind and beautiful in every way beyond the physical. I wanted to give her a home, in me and with me. One day, I'd even marry her, give her my last name too.

My dad never stuck around, so my name never carried weight to me, but I sure would be a prouder man if she carried it. I would act in a way that honored that name. I would protect that name and give it life.

Hopefully, I'd get to see her walking down the aisle, in a long white dress coming toward me. I'd be the luckiest man in the world because she is truly amazing. I wanted to get her a home, like my father never did for my mother.

Four walls can only make a house
And a house is a home without the love and warmth that you set into its bones
The walls I've surrounded myself with have been nothing more than diaries
Blank sheets to keep my fears
A place where I housed ideas of better things, far from here
A window to look toward the future
A stoop that separated me from the real world
And a fence that must have stopped me
Who knew that a home could be so close
That four walls could be transformed
From paper to a shield
Who knew that windows were to let the light in while we danced to our song
And the stoop was for sipping coffee as the sun rises in the morning
Who knew the fence was for holding vines and flowers
Who knew that in order to get home, we just needed the right things
The right hand to help paint the walls
The right shoulder to lean on after unpacking
The right muscle to push the couch in place
Where we would sit with each other after a long day

The right curtains to frame the world as we can see
Who knew I just never had the right key.

"I can't see a thing over these boxes, I can't wait until moving day," Noah said through his teeth. It was a jungle of cardboard in here, and each tower was labeled by where the contents would reside.

It was different, putting two homes worth of stuff into one. I had lived with someone before, but I didn't remember it feeling like a home. Today, I was one step into the door, just a few hours even having a key, and it already felt warm.

The first thing I unpacked was the speakers, so we could play music as we unpacked. Boxes with my handwriting sitting right beside his handwriting, none of our spoons matched, the sheets were different, and the living room décor wasn't even the same color theme. I held up my bright sun-colored frames next to his sports posters.

"Maybe we should just start fresh on some things," I suggested that we go to the store that weekend and pick out decorations together. It would be the first thing in our home that was ours. Not my bathroom decorations paired with his shower curtain, but our frames hung in the living room.

Our couch that was picked out in compromise to both of our likings. When we tested them out, we envisioned which spot on the couch would be mine and which would be his. Was this the optimal size for when we want to lie down and watch a movie?

Would he comfortably fit with me lying on his chest? Did the color suit the off chance that one of us may spill something on it? Eventually, we found the perfect, L-shaped couch.

Noah's long legs needed a place to stretch out, while I was able to stretch in the opposite direction. We fit perfectly on this one.

When you walked into the door of our home, a 4-bedroom on a not-too-crowded street, you would see arched doorways that brought you to each room. Cream-colored walls and large windows kept it bright and warm.

The marbled countertops were offset with a green coffee maker nestled in the corner. A knife block and canisters labeled with *sugar* and *flour* were on the right side of the under mounted sink.

In the middle of the kitchen, the island was littered with chopped produce. Sliced bananas, strawberries, mangoes, pineapple, cucumber, and a sprig of mint. All of which were intended to go into a smoothie.

Rather than a formal dining table, we enjoyed our meals at the small breakfast nook, right by the window. Our home was beginning to look put together and soon enough, lived in. Even the messes here looked better than the messes in my single apartment.

Over time, you would find a slate gray and white backsplash to offset the dark in the marble. The kitchen set was of white dishes and gold-colored utensils, with wooden serving bowls and utensils.

There would be a minimum of one plant in every room because the greenery was lively. More time would pass and the home grew warmer, more cohesive of our two personalities, and more inviting to new memories.

***

A few months had passed now since we'd moved in together. A routine had been set and there were no boxes in sight. Noah usually got home in the evening before I did, so he started our dinner unless we chose to eat out, I'd try to even out the duties by cooking dinner on the weekends.

By the time I got home, I arrived with enough time to help with plating our meals. I swooped up the plates and utensils for cleaning after we were done, while he wiped down the table.

Any leftovers from dinner became our lunches for the next day. It was simple, but beautiful. Our everyday life was the contrast to the overwhelming demand of whatever existed outside the walls of our home. Each day still felt new and exciting, but it also felt real.

Not like a puppy love, or a honeymoon phase, but a knee-deep love that you found only by braving the waters. I knew that my feelings were reciprocated when I said that everything in this home was most important, that this family—the one we're creating from the strands of our heart—was our priority.

I knew in my gut that this was right and there wasn't anywhere else I was supposed to be. I loved him that same way I had since day one, but without the fear of him not loving me back. I think I love him even more because now we have this beautiful, safe home.

Here, nothing bad had ever happened, and nothing bad ever would. Should we face trials, we'd face them together. Should we fail, we'd try again together.

I was confident in this love, I was trusting in this love, and I was invested in my life with my love.

It felt like a lifetime since I had met Hazel, and at the same time, it felt like I hadn't had enough moments with her to yet feel fulfilled. We had grown so much over the years together.

From our skepticism toward love, we grew into new, refreshed eyes that helped us see so much truth in each other. I remember having the urge to say I love you stuck at the tip of my tongue, and now, it flowed effortlessly because it had willing and loving lips to land on.

Lips that never forget to say I love you too. Through tears and confusion, we fixed the world together. There was no more Noah without a Hazel, and I was okay with that. The past that I held on to as a lesson didn't matter to me anymore.

Hazel didn't feel the need to reiterate her past life, she didn't say things to remind me that she was healing from something still—whether that was because she felt safe enough to let the memories rest, or because she felt that I understood and was there, I don't know.

But all that mattered to me was that she felt safe enough to live in the moment with me. We dreamed of a future, but we never dwelled in the past.

The kitchen was cleaned, the living room was tidy, and the laundry was folded and put away. A candle was lit on the dresser in the opposite side of the room and Side B of the current vinyl had just begun. I loved that we can be whole and present in this moment, because here, in our home, the moments became magical.

Vanilla and lavender flowed through the air and created an inviting space on our bed. Hazel walked by to return something to its space, and my hand reached for hers. I caught her mid-stride and gently pulled her to me.

I told her I loved her and kissed her deeply, to which she said, "I love you too." No other words needed to hang in the room, so I kissed her again and felt her rise on her tip toes to kiss me back.

My hand found the twists of her curls, as her hands caressed the back of my neck. To be in this space with her was all that I could ever ask for. I motioned us to the end of bed and took a seat, and Hazel straddled her legs on each side of me.

I can feel the lace rim of her nightgown rising high on her thighs. I had my hands swimming in her curls and hers were around my face as we kissed deeply. Every time we made love, it felt better than the last.

Hazel's arms rose as she removed her clothing, allowing me to kiss her breasts. And I admired her beauty and kissed every part that I could; her neck, her ribs, her stomach, her thighs, and her thighs some more.

She lay down on the bed while I tasted her—sweet and wet—my hands gripped her legs. I could see that she was gripping at the sheets, breathing heavily, but still soft. Within each other, we found solace.

We found solace in the music, in the candlelight, in the lovemaking, and in our home. *We gained everything the day we met.*

***

We lay under the sheets, skin to skin with smiles on our faces. As the air refilled in our lungs, and Hazel's head was on my chest, she said to me, "you love me in the exact way I have always needed love. And I don't know how you do that but damn, I'm happy you do that."

I pulled her closer to me in response; this girl was my everything. Really and truly, I knew this for a fact. "You're mine forever, right babe?" she questioned with a silly smile.

"You know it, baby girl. Today, tomorrow, forever, and ever. When I'm old and can't feed myself. Senile and smelly. I'm all yours." I laughed in return and kissed her smile.

It had been 1,715 days of being in a world where Hazel existed. I had seen her at her lows, so deep that I've had to wade through the waters of her tears to bring her to shore, to bring her home to me.

I had seen her smile shine brighter than every constellation she'd ever pointed out to me. I had seen her sleep peacefully and again, sleep exhaustedly. Surely, I'd not seen every kaleidoscope color that she embodied, but I was so committed to loving her, I would spend my life vowing to press my eye against the canister, continuously turning so I can view every shape, every color and every facet.

She was art in living form, and I was forever entranced. She was kind and wholesome, generous and loving. She had seen me in my worst and angriest form and vowed to love me still.

She'd seen me frustrated and only responded with help. We built plans together with the fabric of our dreams for a life where we both found success. And it was so good with her.

In my pocket, I carried what would lead to my future, my happily ever after. Because I found the girl, and today I wanted her to know that she was the picture I hung in my mind of what the future held for me.

I had a long day ahead of me, so I had to head out early that morning. I sent Hazel a quick message and asked her to return the library books for me, I didn't want them to be past due. Of course, these books came home, but the pages never saw me. Once again, I'd never finished the story and again, the librarian never had to know.

I had so many things to tend to first, but she didn't need to know the details of my busy day, and to my luck, she didn't ask. She was happy to help where I needed her to and agreed to drop them off later that day.

I went to the coffee shop on 3rd and Salem, they had the best coffee, and my day allowed enough time for it before I needed to stop at the library. I'm not sure why Noah continued to check out multiple books, because I know he doesn't read them all.

But I do like his persistence and effort, always saying he will. I doubt he'd ever finish a library find, but I don't share that with him. Instead, we go to the library, and he picks too many books and I ask him to let me know how it turns out, with a smile on my face.

My heart felt like it was going to burst out of my chest, it was heavy and fluttery at the same time. Flowers; check. Music; check. Haircut. Shit, I forgot to get my haircut, too late for that now.

Make sure the outside book deposit drop-box was sealed; check. Ring; check. When Hazel arrived at the library, the one we met at, she would be forced to walk inside to return the books (that actually had a full week before they were deemed late).

She would walk inside to find what I hoped was the happiest day of her life. I just wanted it to be perfect. My palms were sweaty, letting me know that I was more nervous than I imagined. I was pacing back and forth, thinking and thinking of what to say.

*Hazel, from the moment I saw you. Hazel, I love you beyond—Hazel, you are—*frustrated because I sounded so stupid and cliché and couldn't get my thoughts straight. I took a few shallow breaths.

I pulled the ring out of my pocket, intending to take a look at the rose gold band. It was an emerald cut diamond in the center surrounded by a halo. It was vibrant, but timeless.

I expect she'd be here soon, so I was fidgeting more than usual. With a bouquet of mixed flowers in one hand, I tried to pry the box open with just my fingers in the other hand. In every way opposite of smooth, I managed to drop the flowers on the library floor, and the arrangement seemingly spilled at my feet.

I hurriedly kneel down to pick up the lilies, roses and sunflowers, when a perfectly manicured hand extended a peony to me. I looked up and recognized that beautiful smile.

With a small stack of books in one hand and my iced coffee in another, I entered the library to find Noah dressed so handsomely. I can tell he was deep in thought by the furrowed brow lines that decorated his forehead at the moment.

Just then, I saw his feet come to a stop as he failed to juggle something in his hands. Before I knew it, there were flowers everywhere. I made my way to his side, as I would do any time, any place, and any day.

I reached for the most beautiful flower I'd ever seen, "what are you doing here?" I smiled at him as I gave him back his flower. His eyes grew wide with shock to see me, not because he wasn't expecting me, but maybe for another reason that I can't pinpoint just yet because all of these different factors that didn't make sense yet.

He was at the library, but he had asked me to come here today because he didn't have the time. He was surrounded by a clumsy pool of flowers, and he looked to be a nervous, handsome mess. But just as the day we met, clumsy had worked for us.

"Shit, you weren't supposed to see this part," I said with a smile. Of course, once again, I wasn't smooth or graceful. And as much effort as I put into this evening, I wasn't put together either. Her smile was so beautiful though, I could feel my heart steadying. She'd always had that effect on me.

That nervous, crooked smile has had my heart since the day we met in this very library. Being here with him, in this moment, brought me back to that day. It was as if this was always meant to happen, and the path we went down to get here has been nothing short of amazing.

I remained crouched to the floor, surrounded by what's left of the flowers as Noah seemingly swallowed a lump in his throat. My heart seemed to know what was happening before my mind could follow along.

He extended his hand, and suddenly, I remembered the first moment he reached out to shake mine. I was confused the first time we met because he was a stranger, but right now, he extended what felt like more than just his hand, but maybe his whole heart.

He was certainly not a stranger anymore, he was every bit as home as the safe place we left this morning, where he had kissed me before he began his day.

Leaving the flowers on the floor and ignoring the people around us, we were both kneeling on the ground, it was a world of our own. I took in her beauty; lightly coiled curls that came loose from her high ponytail and framed her face.

She was wearing a beautiful yellow sundress that tied at the shoulders and smelled of eucalyptus. Her face was glowing, like always. The words began to spill, like I never needed to practice in the first place.

"There are no words grand enough to properly describe the love that I have for you. There are no colors as beautiful as the life you've painted for me. And there's no sound sweeter than hearing you say that you love me."

"Hazel, I'm a better man for having been loved by you. Every day we wake up, and I get to lie beside you, I'm reminded of my *why.* Why I want to be a better man, why I want to strive for a better life, why I want to give you the world."

"It was here, the first time I ever laid eyes on you, your smile caught me off guard and I've been hooked ever since." Her beautiful smile is looking back at me, tears forming in the corners of her deep eyes.

"It was under the stars that I knew you meant more to me. Like you just illuminated the corners of my mind and have lit up my world ever since. It was finding you in tears that day that made me realize how much I just want to hold you and protect you."

"It's been every single midnight talk, 2am laugh, afternoon smile, and good morning kiss that has made me fall in love with you."

Her head begins to hang on to the words I say as tears reluctantly fall to the library floor. Maybe a seed will take root here as her happy tears water the flowers around us. This space will be our garden forever.

My hand reached for her cheek, a warmth I can't live without, and raised her gaze to meet mine. Because when I ask her, I want her to look into my eyes, so she sees there is no wavering, there is no fear, and there is no question.

I wanted her to see how steady I was in my words. Now with her hand atop mine, we were in the middle of the library. Fallen flowers and bystanders surrounded us as we both remained kneeling down.

Despite the people looking, the hands being held and the embracing happening as they witnessed our love unfolding in the very place we met, my eyes were on her, and hers on me. It felt like we were the only people in the world. Yet, faint whispers played like music in the background as I pulled a small square box out of my pocket.

"Baby, I love you, more than you will ever know. Will marry me?"

My heart is doing flips right now, tears fall down my face and my mind is racing. My heart communicated what was happening to my brain and it felt like I flew into his arms. There was a box, but I didn't hesitate long enough to see what was inside.

It was his words that captured me in this moment. It was the smell of a garden that entranced me. It was holding onto his hand that grounded me. As quickly as my arms were now around him, the tears flooded my cheeks.

I felt the heat rushing to my cheeks, and I'm certain I was as pink as the flowers. He was everything I never thought I'd have. And at the same time, everything I knew I deserved. I could feel how deeply he loved me every time he held me.

There wasn't a doubt in my mind as I replied through my tears of joy, "yes," punctuated with a kiss. "Yes, baby!" Punctuated with a smile, hands embracing each side of his beautiful, crooked smile, "yes, yes, yes," punctuated with sniffles, trying to stop the tears.

Applause filled the room, people were clapping and celebrating our love. Tears streamed down my face, but I had never been happier. We could feel the love surrounding us, the people's whispers became claps, then they became cheers, and finally became congratulations!

I stayed here, in this moment, kneeling on the library floor with the love of my life. The color of lilies, roses, and peonies painted the moment. The sounds of the others dulled as I brought my ear back to Noah.

"I get to be your wife." A smile hung on my lips, which he received so gracefully with a kiss.

"And I get to be your husband," he said with full reciprocation.

"I love you."

"I love you, too."

I slid the ring on her delicate finger, and I was relieved that I got the size correct. It looked great on her finger as she went back and forth between looking at it with her hand down and fingers stretched out, and again with her hand in the air.

She kissed my cheeks and told me, "It's so beautiful!" as tears continued down her face. She hugged me, and then turned her body to me, as if we were sitting on our couch at home.

She must have felt that we were in our own world because we were still on the floor of the library, comfy as ever, and happily engaged. As the moment wore, we collected the flowers and made our way home.

Everyone was saying congratulations as we left and both of us had wide smiles on our faces. We arrived here separately, but decided we would come back for one of the cars tomorrow, so that we could leave together.

At this point, the day is still early, so when we got home, we first began by placing the flowers into a vase and turning the music as loud as we can. Hazel danced in the living room and jumped on the couch, bouncing along to the beat.

She motioned for me to join her, when I put my drink on the counter and with a wide smile, walked over to my wife-to-be.

She jumped into my arms and wrapped her legs around me, and we spun to the sound of the music before she was down to her tip toes, kissing me. Our song came on, and we danced in the living room for the entire duration.

I love to hear the way you love me
And I love to hear the reasons why you'd never leave
Desert me
Or deplete me
I love to hang on to the words you hung in your mind with
which you created me
So, I love to love you same
And paint you with words that I plucked from the sky
I looked up to the stars and begged
Reason with me
Give me something as beautifully made as the man that
stands before me
Cause I love the way he loves me, see
So, I need to find something to adorn his smile with
Because his loving is the kind of love that is ever so
deserving
It's powerful in a way that reminded me I was nurturing
So, I want to gift him a love that is forever nourishing
Cause I love the way he loves me, see
I love the way he loves me seen
I love the way he loves me in dream
I love the way he loves me in between
Minutes and seconds and hours of daylight
Sunrays as they pass through the blinds, and gleam

I love the way he loves me in my sheets
I love the way he loves me
You see?
So, I need words that fit him
To gift him
Words that are just as loving.

It feels good to be this whole
All the pieces finally fit
In this cavern of my chest
Breathing is easier
And questioning comes less
I'm grounded in a way that I never knew to be true
Planted, in a way
Rooted deep within the earth of you
Blooming life, getting ready to birth a new chapter with you
Blooming life, getting ready to birth a brighter view
Planted, in a way
That I surround myself with garden views
Roses in your eyes
And sunflowers in the touch of you, velvet smooth
Daisies in your kiss
And every exchange is the chance to reminisce
How I fell for you
September felt like home, because like the leaves
I was falling too
Never afraid of the descent
Because I knew it was only a matter of time till I'd be green
again
You always seemed to make me new
The winters never bothered me

Because I was always warm with you
Back to springtime we'd come
Just as I could trust in you
I'd be blooming soon
And summer was always magic with you
When stars would shoot across the sky
Cheering for us as they flew by
Writing our names in the highlights
To be whole is the only way to describe the feeling that
we've made
All the seasons of you, mix perfectly with mine
And I wonder if that's why they call it nature
Because you and I are the perfect example of such a natural
love
I'm more me and grounded then I ever was
I'm more blue skies and clouds
Breezes and birds chirping
Summer rays and summer rain
Than I've ever been before
I never questioned the effort in planting the seeds of us
Because I trusted so deeply that we'd reap what we sow
That from our inception as a unit
We created a cycle so reliable
That the stars looked to us for guidance
And that's why I feel so whole.

There are wisps of angels in the air
Sending messages to eyes and ears
To let them know they're never alone
They say things like *it's okay to breathe now*
Place a light feathered hand on your shoulder
Forcing the tension from you
They say *changes are coming*
Giving you a new canvas to paint your murals on
Because your life has been art
Art in the sense that colors contrast
Allowing you to see love from malice
Art in the sense that you learned how to draw firm lines
And called them boundaries
Art in the sense that the biggest parts of admiration were found in the shadows of you
Art in the sense that though it may have been a dark painting
You learned to be a loving admirer of the view
9:26 on the clock again, and again, and again
The angels flood you like ice cold water down your itchy throat
Another day is done
But there's a new canvas
A mural waiting to be drawn

The angels must be singing again

It's 9:26pm

Changes are coming and I close my eyes to wait for the new dawn.

I was so scared to tell him, even though he had been a part of my life for 7 years now, and had never let me down, I was terrified to tell him. I must have had butterflies in my stomach, a quick internet search told me that I would feel that at some point.

***

It was a few weeks ago, I was hysterical, I couldn't keep my head on straight and I managed to cry every tear that had rented space in my body. I was an emotional wreck—even so—that night, he held me tight and told me how much he loved me.

He reminded me of my worth, the good days and the beauty in the world, running his fingers through my tangled, curly hair. That night, I tossed my regular toss and turn. It was 1:47 in the morning and I found his warmth beside me, I woke up feeling exhausted, but beyond grateful.

I was madly in love with this man, because he was an expression of love even in my worst times—which I always thought I had more of than what he deserved to deal with. I lay back down on my side to face him, placing my hand on his cheek.

His warmth was the very thing that calmed me. I leaned in to give him a gentle kiss and nuzzle closer to him. My tossing and turning must have woken him because he felt my kiss; he felt me close and responded by pulling me closer and kissing me once more.

Tears involuntarily fell past my eyes, to which he responded with another kiss and whispered, "I love you." In the dead of the night, where words hang like stars in the sky, all I needed to hear and all he could say was 'I love you'.

I was grateful for this man, grateful for his lips on mine and his warmth. I was grateful to be loved by him, and small tears continued to travel down my face. Noah kissed my cheek, and then my lips. He kissed my neck as he intertwined our fingers.

My scattered breathing started to steady and became deeper and deeper. Consistent, deep breaths, only broken by kisses, and the only thing I could do was focus long enough to say, "I love you too."

My oversized t-shirt now lay at the foot of the bed. We were skin to skin underneath our sheets, Noah, now on top of me, gentle and firm at the same time. Our kissing became passionate and ravenous, there were no more tears, except the ones pooled on the pillowcase, but those were a thing of the past.

The moment wasn't filled with pain anymore, it was filled with love and lust. In the dead of night, when the world was asleep, Noah and I were one, he made love to me, and I loved him so. He made love to me, and I felt no pain, he made love to me, and I loved him endlessly.

Now he lay down, and I loved him with full reciprocation. My hands found balance planted on his chest, and my hair was a wild mess, but he said, "you're so beautiful," to which I responded with a kiss.

Slowly, I loved him, passionately, I loved him, until we were both moaning. His fingers found home in my hair, stroking and massaging my scalp until my eyes closed. Fluidly, I loved him, with ease, I loved him, with every breath, I loved him.

His hands began to trace the contour of my body; starting with my hair, he then caressed my cheeks to pull me closer to kiss him once more. His hands traveled from the lowest point of my back, up until he reached my ribcage.

As his fingertips explored my body, I whispered, "I love you," in shallow and scattered breathing.

"I love you, too," as his hands cupped my breasts, and my stride changed. On this bed, he and I were on an island, riding waves and soaking wet while swimming seas.

"I love you," became moaning.

"I love you," became, "don't stop."

"I love you," became screaming.

I loved him, endlessly. We made love, back and forth, back and forth, until it could be felt in every cell in our bodies, we made love, until it was felt so intensely that it exceeded our capacity and rushed out in waves.

And I loved him endlessly.

Skin to skin, we lay together and closed our eyes, drifting back to sleep. Wherever he was, would always be my favorite place to be. It was 6:04 and I woke to the sound of my morning alarm. His kiss started my day, and nothing felt heavy anymore.

***

And still, I was terrified to tell him. He had never let me down, but I was scared because this was going to change his life. I'd known for 4 days now, only trying to decide on the perfect way to tell him.

I wanted him to be happy, I wanted him to still love me entirely and even more. So tonight, I'd tell him. I didn't have any fancy or comical reveal, just my words. I planned to make his favorite meal tonight, light a few candles and play some nice songs.

We were sitting at the dinner table and halfway into the meal, this smiling beautiful man suggested some wine. He poured two glasses and wanted to toast to our beautiful life. And I smiled my biggest smile, because we did have such a beautiful life. Everything we'd built together was perfect, but I didn't sip on the wine he had generously poured.

"Did you want white wine, baby?"

"No, honey. I'm okay, thank you though. I actually don't want wine at all. Because I have to tell you something." My heart was beating so hard, I wondered if he could hear it. Without even thinking about it, my thumb was fidgeting with my engagement ring, now paired with a wedding band, spinning them in circles around my finger. My smile, even bigger, was nervous, but genuine.

"Go ahead babe, you know you can tell me anything."

"Well." I paused, the nerves were rushing to my head, so I pushed the words out on what felt like the last of the air in my lungs, "I'm pregnant, we're going to have a baby."

For 63 seconds, he was silent.

63 long seconds of wondering if this was good or bad news.

63 seconds of my heart threatening to burst through my sternum and out of my chest.

"Really? We're going to have a baby?" His eyebrows were raised, with tears caught in his throat, he smiled with a question. "I'm going to be a dad?" and those tears welled in the corners of his eyes.

His smile grew so wide, he got out his chair, lifted me up and spun me in a circle. "We're gonna have a baby! Hazel, you're gonna to be a mom," after gently putting me down, he placed his hands around my face, holding me close, kissing me.

We cried happy tears and I questioned why I was ever scared in the first place. Noah looked me in the eyes, and he said, "Hazel, I promise, that every day going forward, I'm going to love you, and I'm going to appreciate you. I'm going to love this baby, and it's going to have the best home. You and I are going to be parents, and we get to have a family and—"

He paused and kissed me one more time before saying, "I have been wanting this with you for such a long time. From the moment I fell in love with you, I wanted more of you, and I wanted a future with you, and a home with you. Thank you. Hazel, thank you for loving me and trusting me. I love you so much."

This time, I stopped him to kiss him. I stretched up on my tippy toes and wrapped my arms around the back of his neck to get as close to his lips as possible. I kissed him like I had fallen in love with him all over again.

We were going to be parents and I was certain that I had the best partner in the world to become a mom with.

To manifest
Is to allow the universe to hear you so deeply
To love you so fully
That even the stars feel compelled to see to it that you win
It's when the universe conspires to give you what you ask
for
Past the point of wishes
It is a declaration that you are heard and seen
That you are deserving of your dreams
That there is magic in reality
That the bounds of the world unfold miraculously
And somehow I miraculously
Crossed paths with such tenacity
Found myself in another soul, you always matched with me
I bled ten times over, but you managed to capture me
Look after me
Stop the bleed
And heal me
You managed to calm me
Understand my dreams
Comprehend the different aspects of me
And light up the darkness in between
You managed to be the very thing I never knew I was
manifesting

I said I'd get safety, stable, and whole
But little did I know
That would come in the shape of you
The soft lips of you
The warmth of you
Little did I know that I was manifesting you
I feel so safe knowing that you're here
Because after all the late-night discussions consulting with
the stars
You appear, here in my arms
And I know that this is what they conspired for
I blinked and we were knee-deep in our forever
Time moved faster than light it seemed
One year later and the soundtrack of our home was the
excitement of tiny toes and fingers
A love that even I couldn't have imagined we could make
But here, she looks back up at us, and I see a mini-Hazel
I knew God heard me that night, because I was holding an
Angel
Life would never be the same and I never wanted to
experience another day without the two loves of my life
Another three years pass and my wife says, "It's time."
We rush to the hospital at 2:55
She's beautiful, and so strong
And by 5:28am, she exclaims, "baby, he has your eyes!"
Tears fill the room, but life only grew brighter
Beside our children, a puppy sits beside them
They walk, run and play together
And life grows more fun
Their joy echoes in the hallways
Life was beautiful these days

I blinked, and we were knee-deep in forever
Feels like I have the whole world, and no could convince
me of anything that could come after
Grateful is an understatement
I feel so deeply for the view that I have now in life
I feel so strongly for the mishaps that happened along the
way and the sadness that once sat at my side
They say everything happens for a reason
And rather than asking why me, I know why now
I know why it took so long for me to get here
Why I endured the pain that I felt along the way
I know why I failed in love time and time again
I know why everything was constantly changing
Because now I can appreciate more
I appreciate the urgency of time, and respect it in its need to
move slow
I appreciate the delicacy of waiting, because if it weren't for
those moments in between, we wouldn't have had all that
space to place a foundation
I appreciate the quiet because I can fully hear my heart
calling to yours
I appreciate the dark because now I can feel just how warm
the light really is
I appreciate everything that wasn't there before, because I
look at life now and see it for so much more
Those moments that once lingered, stagnant in the air
Are now spaces in time to cherish, to love why I'm here
I blinked, and we were knee-deep in forever
I could swim here
I could bask in this river.

As I lay there, with this man by my side and our small children taking up much more of the bed than they should, I found myself gazing out the window. The sun was shining through the rose bushes that we had planted together.

That day was hot and humid, and still we found smiles in the labor. There was love tangled in the roots of the rose bushes, planted, and then watered with laughter. Noah and I had built a home here, within each other and from scratch.

He was a foolish boy when we met and today, a man stood before me. I was a young, naive girl with my head down, but Noah picked me up by the chin and showed me beauty in everything.

In the mundane, in the ugly, in the new, there was beauty in life, and it was made more beautiful being shown through his lens.

It was early Saturday morning and the sun was peeking through the blinds after cutting through the bushes. Roses illuminating, shadows dancing on the bedroom walls. I loved it here. I remembered when I had fought tooth and nail against the prospect of love.

I was so certain that it came with destruction at the end of it and I would never fall victim to that again. But I loved it here. He showed me that love wasn't what I thought it was, I think that was what made me love him the most.

We took the time with each other and didn't rush into anything. I accepted him for who he was at the time, and he did the same for me. That was the most important part, there were no expectations for who we should be, we were allowed to be our most authentic self with each other.

From there, we chose love, and we chose it for a lifetime. Without his patience and kindness, I'd never be here, surrounded by rose bush shadows dancing along the walls as the children's laughter mixed with my husband's.

To be Mrs. Noah Anderson, was like my dreams had come true somewhere along the road. *And it was perfect.*

Epilogue

Hazel and Noah became a dream. They started out as moments in time, where I hoped I could rewrite history. They started out as characters who had the happy ending that people deserved and ended up being the dream I sought to manifest.

They are the understanding in the lifelong reactions to pain that's been held for so long.

They are the slow dances in the most hectic of moments.

They are the lyrics to a melody that you save in a playlist for one-day vows.

They are the small sliver of hope that I keep tucked under my pillow.

If I ever wake to a new life with the name of Hazel, I can only hope to find my Noah.